LIBERATING the SOUL

A GUIDE FOR SPIRITUAL GROWTH
Volume five

By
Shaykh Nazim Adil Al-Haqqani

Foreword By
Shaykh Muhammad Hisham Kabbani

ISLAMIC SUPREME COUNCIL OF AMERICA

Library of Congress Cataloging-in-Publication Data

Naqshbandi, Muhammad Nazim Adil al-Haqqani, 1922-
Liberating the soul : a guide for spiritual growth / by Shaykh Nazim Adil al-Haqqani.
1st ed.
Washington, DC : Islamic Supreme Council of America, <2002-2005 >
v. <1-3> ; 23 cm.

Subjects: Sufism. Naqshaband⁻iyah.
Series: Sufi wisdom series
BP189 .N368 2002 297.4 21

2002109747

Published and Distributed by:
Islamic Supreme Council of America

17195 Silver Parkway, #401
Fenton, MI 48430 USA
Tel: (888) 278-6624
Fax:(810) 815-0518
Email: staff@naqshbandi.org
Web: http://www.naqshbandi.org

First Edition July 2006
ISBN: 1-930409-33-8

Shaykh Nazim Adil al-Haqqani (right) with his disciple of fifty years, Shaykh Muhammad Hisham Kabbani. Head of the world's largest Naqshbandi Sufi spiritual order, Shaykh Nazim is known for his life-altering lessons in how to discipline the ego, reach a state of spiritual surrender, and achieve true liberation from the bondage of worldly distraction and pursuit. Shaykh Hisham Kabbani, Shaykh Nazim's deputy, accompanies the venerable shaykh on his many visits to various regions of the world, where they meet with political and religious leaders, media, and throngs of common folk.

table of contents

fOREWORD

Bismillahi-r-Rahmani-r-Rahim
In the Name of Allah, the Most Beneficent, the Most Merciful

All praise is due to God Almighty, Allah the Exalted and Bounteous. And praise and blessings be upon His perfect servant, the exemplar to humankind and mercy to all creation, Prophet Muhammad 繫,[1] and on his family and Companions.

This fifth in the series, *Liberating the Soul,* is another wonderful compendium of *sohbets* or spiritual discourses by our master, the chief of saints and reviver of the prophetic way, the *Sunnah,* in an age of materialism; the teacher of millions and worldwide leader of the Naqshbandi-Haqqani Sufi Order, Mawlana Shaykh Muhammad Nazim Adil al-Haqqani, may Allah grant him bountiful health and a long life.

In past times, the living Sufi shaykh and saints never accepted a student or follower before completing his Islamic law and jurisprudence, memorizing the entire Quran, and knowing Islamic law, *Shari'ah,* from beginning to end. Then and only then, would the shaykh give them *bay'ah* (initiation) for at that time they know they are sound.

In the past everyone had to study religious knowledge. This was going on until recently. In the past, wherever a parent raised a child—whether on the subcontinent, the Middle East, or the East, where most of the saints are living—their focus was that their children grow up and study the basic structure of Islam. This was their higher education. If you look into history, this was the educational system and whatever other subjects or sciences that were directly related to it. So these people were given a complete understanding before they took initiation from a shaykh.

---

[1] 繫 stands for *"Salla-Lahu 'alayhi wa sallam,"* meaning, "Allah's peace and blessings be upon him," the Islamic invocation for Prophet Muhammad 繫.

All people entering a Sufi path, *tariqah*, knew what the Sufi saints required and they were coming to the shaykh only after they had graduated. Then they sought to achieve the spiritual aspect of the faith in addition to its discipline. After they finished the physical dimension, they sought the *haqiqah* dimension - Reality. At that time they were more powerful because the knowledge of Reality does not change the external (*Shari'ah*) knowledge but rather gives it support.

Today no one is seeking such knowledge. Now, everyone is seeking the knowledge of science. In this era, in this century, the educational system is focusing on science, computers, and so on. Although both parties are going to die and they will not take that science with them to the grave, the party that took the knowledge of Reality will receive something beneficial because they took something that is eternal.

Today people's focus is scattered. So now, the Sufis and especially the Naqshbandi-Haqqani line, which is a direct chain to the Prophet 鷺 through the lineage of the Grandshaykh, have relaxed the restrictions and requirements to enter *tariqah*.

Since the time of the Prophet 鷺 we know that in spirituality, knowledge is always rising. Knowledge is always growing. It is impossible, like in any science, for knowledge to stop; it is always on the increase.

In the Naqshbandi understanding, spirituality is always ascending, because the Prophet's 鷺 knowledge is continuously ascending. Moreover, as the Prophet 鷺 is ascending, all other prophets are ascending and so too are all *awliya* ascending, because scholars and saints are inheritors of the prophets. They move with them. Therefore, from one centuty to the next that knowledge is ever-increasing and more new things are coming.

Therefore, in understanding the spirituality of Islam, our grandshaykh used to say that in the past the meaning of *tariqah* was obedience. But today the meaning of *tariqah* is love, because not everyone can obey today. Our Grandshaykh said that in this time nobody has the ability to obey or listen, therefore, what would be the benefit of *tariqah* if it was still based on obedience? For that reason the manifestations that are coming from the Divine Presence, by the intermediation of the Prophet 鷺 has changed.

It is enough in this century for the seekers to love, because times are harder. The darkness is more and sinning is more. Therefore, mercy is higher, so as mercy is greater now, only a very thin wire is needed to pull, and it is sufficient. If you keep that connection, you do not need a thick rope now. You need love, because everyone is running, busy with worldly affairs, and not do the spiritual practices. When you do them, you will get that benefit if you are holding the rope.

To make this point clearer, let us say in this house there is a treasure of one hundred gold coins. If anyone comes to pray, these one hundred gold coins are going to be distributed among whomever comes to pray. Therefore, if one hundred people come, each person can take away one. If fifty people come, each person can take two. If only one person comes, he takes all one hundred. Therefore, Allah, God is generous. Whatever He has given, He does not take back. When He gave to His "Ummah"—His humanity—on the Day of Promises, Allah asked His servants, "Who am I and who are you?" They said, "We are Your servants; You are our Lord." He took from them a promise to accept Him and to worship Him. When they said "Yes," He threw on everyone that "money". That treasure is so huge that it encompasses everyone. So the shares meant for all the servants, who today are no longer performing their prayers nor keeping their spiritual practices, are being given to those who <u>are</u> observing them, because that "money" is always coming down.

So now our Grandshaykh said if you maintain a connection to the living shaykh, it is enough—you will be saved. And that is wisdom behind Mawlana Shaykh Nazim (may Allah bless him) giving initiation without restriction, because he knows that today no one is acquainted with *Shari'ah* or Islamic jurisprudence.

In past times, people had no choice; the study of religion was the main curriculum of the educational system. Now religion is no longer part of a "good" education. Religion has been discarded like a dry bone. No one is teaching religion anymore, even in Muslim countries, except to those who earnestly seek it out. Even then it might be one in one thousand of the total population that desire to study religion.

So the wisdom of Allah was that He did not want to leave the *Ummah* (community) without a spiritual connection. So an order came to the *awliya* to give initiation to anyone that asks for it. Even if someone meets the shaykh one time, it is enough; he has been 'hooked'.

Mawlana Shaykh Nazim is one such knower. One sitting with him, even one time, will be 'hooked'. We have truly been fortunate to be able to sit at his feet and to learn, and with his permission to spread the light of his teachings east and west, north and south. Seekers circle the flame of his spiritual light and seek to quench their thirst at the bounteous fountain of his wisdom, which flows unceasingly from his heart

There is fresh fruit and there is plastic fruit. Real fruit has a taste such that when you eat it, its essence is experienced. Plastic fruit has no taste; it has only the appearance of fruit. In like manner, the knowledge and teaching of a shaykh who has been authorized through a chain of saints going back to the Prophet ﷺ will be flavorful. Allah will bestow His mercy and His manifestations on such a person when he is reading the shaykh's words because in doing so, whether he is aware of it or not, he is connected through his heart, through the shaykh to his grandshaykh, and so on up to Sayyidina Abu Bakr as-Siddiq ؓ,[2] and from Sayyidina Abu Bakr ؓ to the Prophet ﷺ.

A real shaykh speaks to people in accordance to their ranks and levels of understanding; as such shaykhs are inheritors of the Prophet Muhammad, who said, "Whosoever wants to teach people must be careful to notice the level of understanding of his audience and to address them accordingly."

Mawlana Shaykh Nazim carries the secret of addressing people at their level of understanding, and that is a manifestation of Allah's tremendous love and mercy to him. Allah has authorized him with that power and authority because he has maintained inimitable sincerity, piety and loyalty to Allah's religion, held fast to every obligation, and honored the Holy Qur'an

---

[2] ؓ stands for *"Radi-Allahu 'anhu/anha,"* the Islamic invocation for the male/female Companions of the Prophet.

and the Prophetic *Sunnah* with the highest respect. He is like all the saints of the Naqshbandi Order before him and like all saints of other orders before him—like his forefathers Sayyidina 'Abdul Qadir Jilani and Sayyidina Jalaluddin Rumi.

Therefore, approach this book with reverence, for it contains precious jewels of guidance and understanding. Know that the words of the knowers are special. One may read them, reread them and reread them yet again, and each time they give a fresh taste and a new understanding. For this reason it is said that the words of the knowers never grow stale. Mawlana Shaykh Nazim's teachings exemplify this characteristic, for if anyone in difficulty or seeking good counsel picks up a volume of his sohbets, immediately, upon opening it to any page, seeking to address the problem at hand, he or she will find the solace and guidance appropriate to his or her problem at that moment. Hence, among the saints, Shaykh Nazim is considered Sahib al-Waqt, "the Man of the Moment," and his teachings are comprehensive, inspiring and appropriate for the people of this time and their conditions.

We humbly present this volume to you as a source of blessing and wisdom.

Shaykh Muhammad Hisham Kabbani
Fenton, Michigan
July 21, 2006

introduction

Endless praise and thanks be to God Most High, who guides His servants to His light by means of other servants of His whose hearts He illuminates with His divine love.

Since the beginning of human history, God Most High has conveyed His revealed guidance to mankind through His prophets and messengers, beginning with the first man, Adam ﷺ. The prophetic line includes such well-known names as Noah, Abraham, Ishmael, Isaac, Jacob, Joseph, Lot, Moses, David, Solomon, and Jesus, peace be upon them all, ending and culminating in Muhammad, the Seal of the Prophets ﷺ, a descendant of Abraham ﷺ, ﷺwho brought the final revelation from God to all mankind.

But although there are no longer prophets upon the earth, the Most Merciful Lord has not left His servants without inspired teachers and guides. *Awliya*—holy people or saints—are the inheritors of the prophets. Up to the Last Day, these "friends of God," the radiant beacons of truth, righteousness and the highest spirituality, will continue in the footsteps of the prophets, calling people to their Lord and guiding seekers to His glorious Divine Presence.

One such inspired teacher, a shaykh or *murshid* of the Naqshbandi Sufi Order, is Shaykh Nazim Adil al-Qubrusi al-Haqqani. A descendant not only of the Holy Prophet Muhammad ﷺ but also of the great Sufi masters 'Abul Qadir Gilani and Jalaluddin Rumi, Shaykh Nazim was born in Larnaca, Cyprus, in 1922 during the period of British rule of the island. Gifted from earliest childhood with an extraordinarily spiritual personality, Shaykh Nazim received his spiritual training in Damascus at the hands of Maulana Shaykh 'Abdullah ad-Daghestani (fondly referred to as "Grandshaykh"), the mentor of such well-known figures as Gurjieff and J. G. Bennett, over a period of forty years.

Before leaving this life in 1973, Grandshaykh designated Shaykh Nazim as his successor. In 1974, Shaykh Nazim went to London for the first time, thus initiating what was to become a yearly practice during the month of Ramadan up to 1990s. A small circle of followers began to grow around him, eagerly taking their training in the ways of Islam and *tariqah* at his hands.

From this humble beginning, the circle has grown to include thousands of *murids* or disciples in various countries of the world, among whom are to be found many eminent individuals, both religious and secular. Shaykh Nazim is a luminous, tremendously impressive spiritual personality, radiating love, compassion and goodness. He is regarded by many of his *murids* as the *qutub* or chief saint of this time.

The shaykh teaches through a subtle interweaving of personal example and talks ("Associations" or *sohbets*), invariably delivered extempore according to the inspirations that are given to him. He does not lecture, but rather pours out from his heart into the hearts of his listeners such know-ledge and wisdoms as may change their innermost beings and bring them toward their Lord as His humble, willing, loving servants.

Shaykh Nazim's language and style are unique, so eloquent, moving and flavorful that not only do his teachings seem inspired but also his extraordinary use of words. His *sohbets* represent the teachings of a twentieth century Sufi master, firmly grounded in Islamic orthodoxy, speaking to the hearts of the seekers of God of any faith tradition from his own great, wide heart, in a tremendous outpouring of truth, wisdom and divine knowledge which is surely unparalleled in the English language, guiding the seeker toward the Divine Presence.

The sum total of Shaykh Nazim's message is that of hope, love, mercy and reassurance. In a troubled and uncertain world in which old, time-honored values have given place to new ones of confused origins and unclear prospects, in which a feeling heart and thinking mind is constantly troubled by a sense of things being terribly disordered and out of control, in which the future seems forebodingly dark and uncertain for humanity, he proclaims God's love and care for His servants, and invites them to give their hearts to Him.

Shaykh Nazim holds out to seekers the assurance that even their smallest steps toward their Lord will not go unnoticed and unresponded to. Rather than threatening sinners with the prospect of eternal Hell, he offers hope of salvation from the Most Merciful Lord, and heart-warming encouragement and incentive for inner change and growth. As one who has traversed every step of the seeker's path and reached its pinnacle, he offers both inner and practical guidelines for attaining the highest spiritual goals.

Volumes One through Five in this series constist of Shaykh Nazim's talks from the Ramadans of 1984 through 1988, while Volume Six consists of a number of talks given on other occasions in various years. Each of these talks is entirely extempore, as Shaykh Nazim never prepares his words but invariably speaks according to inspirations coming to his heart.

In keeping with the shaykh's methodology—the methodology of the prophets, particularly of the Last Prophet, Muhammad, peace be upon him and upon them all, and of the Qur'an itself—of reinforcing vital lessons by repetition and reiteration, the same themes and anecdotes recur again and again. The talks seem to come in unannounced clusters, centering around a primary theme, which develops and evolves according to the spiritual state of the listeners. Thus, Shaykh Nazim may cite the same verse or *hadith*, or tell the same tale on different occasions, each time reinforcing a slightly different aspect of the eternal message of love and light which is Islam.

The shaykh's talks are interspersed with words and phrases from Arabic and other Islamic languages. These are translated either in the text itself, in footnotes the first time they occur, or, for general and recurrent terms, in the Glossary at the end of this volume. Qur'anic verses quoted in the text have been referenced for easy access.

Every attempt has been made to retain the shaykh's original language with minimal editing. However, since these talks were transcribed from audio tapes recorded on amateur equipment by listeners for their own personal use (or, in the case this volume, by a *murid* extremely familiar with the shaykh's language and ideas, by hand), some inadvertent errors may have found their way into the text. For these, we ask Allah's forgiveness and your kind indulgence. May He fill your heart with light and love as you read and reflect upon these inspired words, and guide you safely to His exalted Divine Presence.

publisher's note

Shaykh Nazim is fluent in Arabic, Turkish and Greek, and semi-fluent in Engish. Over three decades, his llectures have been transated into twenty or more languages, and to date have reached the furthest corners of the globe. We sincerely hope the reader will appreciate the author's unique language style, which has been painstakingly preserved in this work.

As some of the terms in this book may be foreign, to assist the reader we have provded transliterations, as well as a detailed glossary.

notes

The following symbols are universally recognized and have been respectfully included in this work:

The symbol 鐮 represents *sall-Allahu 'alayhi wa sallam* (Allah's blessings and greetings of peace be upon him), which is customarily recited after reading or pronouncing the holy name of Prophet Muhammad 鐮.

The symbol 鐮 represents *'alayhi 's-salam* (peace be upon him/her), which is customarily recited after reading or pronouncing the holy names of the other prophets, family members of Prophet Muhammad 鐮, the pure and virtuous women in Islam, and the angels.

The symbol 鐮/鐮 represents *radi-Allahu 'anhu/ 'anha* (may Allah be pleased with him/her), which is customarily recited after reading or pronouncing the holy names of Companions of the Prophet 鐮.

In the Name of Allah, The Beneficent and The Munificent

This, my English, is strange English. Not everyone can understand because, *subhanallah*, meanings are coming to my heart, and when running in my heart to give to you, I am using any means – from here, from there - bringing any word which may be useful.

I am like a person waiting for water to run out from the faucet. Then, when suddenly it comes, and he knows the water is going to be turned off, stop running, he may take any container – with a no-good shape, broken on one side, or anything he may find there – quickly bringing them to take that water and store it. Therefore, when meanings are coming to my heart, I am trying to explain with any word, which you may understand or not. But you must understand, because we have a saying, "Listeners must be more wise than speakers." Therefore, when inspiration comes, we must explain.

They are living words, not plastic – bananas, plastic; apples, plastic, and grapes. Even if the shapes are not much, they are living, real. When you are going to arrange them in measures, good system; when you are going to be engaged by outside forms, you are losing meanings. ▲

1: training ourselves for servanthood

By the name of Allah, All-Mighty, All-Merciful, Most Beneficent and Most Munificent.

We are thanking Allah Almighty that He is giving us another chance to reach Ramadan, the fasting month, the most valuable and most lighted, most radiant month. And we are asking from Allah Almighty to grant us inspirations. We in need, and He has endless knowledge, wisdoms and divine Favor Oceans.

If we are asking according to our souls' desires, He should give to us. Sometimes it is easy to give to us. Sometimes there is present, among the attenders, those who are asking deeply, and we are giving pearls and deep meanings, and some [other] times we are giving only shells. And Allah wants from His servants to ask as much as they are able. When He gives, it is never going to be less for Him.

Sometimes I was in Mecca and Medina and Jerusalem, and I was asking, "When are you going to make Quds, Jerusalem, free?"

When are Muslims going to be free? They are slaves to their egos and as long as they are slaves to their egos, it is delayed for Quds to be freed, the *qiblah* for all nations,[1] and also for Muslims.

For everything there must be some reason; nothing happens without a reason. Muslims are egos' slaves now and are following their egos' desires.

---

[1]When the command to observe prayers was revealed to the Prophet 饜, he and the Muslims prayed facing Jerusalem. It was not until the second year after the Prophet's emigration to Medina that the *qiblah* was changed from Jerusalem to Mecca by divine revelation, as commanded in Qur'an, 2:142-150.

Therefore, Quds, which was for fourteen centuries under the hands of Muslims, now is taken from them. *He* is making us to think about our freedom!

People may say that earlier Muslims were slaves. And now there are so many Islamic countries but they are *all* slaves. But when we are going to be slaves to the Lord, Almighty Allah, everything is going to be easy.

Subhanallah, He is making a way to enter [the subject]; I was asking for inspirations. They are making me free to move in any direction, as They like, not bounded; as long as you are giving your attention, it is easy to give us inspirations. "O Nazim Efendi, ask for yourself and for those who are attending with you," said Grandshaykh. "We are not heedless of you, what you are intending. You are under our eyes. *Ask if they are created to be servants or to be kings.*"

Everyone must ask himself if he is created to be a servant or to be a king. But now everyone is asking to be a king. The Prophet ﷺ declared in his holy *hadith*, saying, "The lord of people, the master of people, is the one who is a servant to them, not that one who is asking to be served. The one who gives himself to serve people, he is going to be a master."

This is for all people, the most famous and most valuable measure of humanity. People now are following ways to establish humanism. But they must use firstly *that* measure: to teach people to be servants to mankind, to make themselves to be servants. If anyone does not like to be a servant, no humanism.

The Seal of the Prophets, Muhammad ﷺ, gives honor to those who are servants. For everything, the one who is serving is going to be more acceptable in the community and in the Divine Presence. And we must try to teach ourselves to be servants.

Man is created to be a servant, firstly to his Lord. Even kings and queens, heads of communities, have been ordered also to be servants to their Lord.

3

This country is a kingdom. That is the best system of ruling, the noblest system, more honored for nations than republics. As the Prophet 寒 said, after kings will come tyrants and dictators. England is a kingdom, and therefore I am asking Allah to keep that kingdom on this island because that kingdom gives us our freedom, even though we are not Christians—more freedom than our Muslim countries give. Allah may ask me about that on the Day of Judgment.

I am advising every Muslim to thank Allah for Her Majesty the Queen, asking Him to keep her on His right path and to make her happy, here and Hereafter. Her Majesty the Queen is the chief of the Church of England. It means that she is accepting to be the servant of the Lord, Almighty Allah.

Even kings are honored by being servants to Almighty; no higher rank than that, even for kings and queens. And common people also have a chance for the same rank, to be servants to the Lord, Almighty Allah. I am asking to be a humble servant to Him. He honored all mankind by being servants to Him Almighty; we have been given a grant, to be slaves to Him. I don't think that Her Majesty the Queen is refusing to be a slave to her Lord, Almighty Allah.

But are we looking at that point during our lives or not? Even believers are not thinking about it. If they were, this world would be changed, quickly; from evening up to morning, it would be changed to another view. Very few people are waking up and thinking that they are servants, and washing and worshipping—very few. And Allah, during the nighttimes, when the stars are shining, is looking at His servants, but they are sleeping or dancing. And He likes His servants, during the nights, to be with Him, even for a short while. The King of Kings is making His servants to awaken, but we are turning from one side to the other, not thinking that He is looking at us, to be with Him!

Daytimes we are too busy with something very cheap; we are making ourselves busy with the cheapest things. A person is running after stones, to fill sacks, but on the other side there are diamonds. Who is busy—the one filling them with diamonds and pearls and emeralds, or the one taking stones?

First-standard-minded people may understand me; too clever ones may read other books and go to scholars. So many sacks of stones—and I am asking to take diamonds but we are busy with stones. All Muslims, also, all people, are occupied by business; on their heads is written "Business-man," to make those stones more and more. And Allah is pouring pearls and diamonds on His servants, saying, "Come and serve yourself and take!"

Days are running to an end; don't think you are here permanently. Think about that; try to be a servant to Allah first. Don't be worried about business. We don't need business, we need servanthood. If people want this world to be Paradise, they can make it Paradise. Serve, firstly, the Lord; secondly, mankind. Then all troubles and miseries will be finished.

When Allah created our souls and gathered all peoples' souls and then clothed them in their forms,[2] He made a show of every kind of job, profession. Everything was there. Then He ordered all people, saying, "Everyone may choose for himself that one which is suitable for himself."

Then all of them said, "This is for me," each one taking something. Only one group of people did not choose anything.

And Allah asked, "Why are you not choosing?"

They said, "O our Lord, our choice is *You*. We choose to be Your servants, O our Lord!"

And Allah answered, swearing by His divinity, saying, "And I am your Lord. If you choose My service, I will make all people servants to you."

Whoever chooses to be a servant to his Lord first, his ego is going to be a servant to him. Then your ego may carry you from East to West in a moment, with miraculous power. The earth may be gold by your look; every part of creation is going to be a servant to you. *Fatehah!* ▲

---

[2]That is, on the Day of Promises in the spiritual world, mentioned in 7:172.

2: preparing ourselves to carry out orders and face our destiny

You can find everything in the Holy Qur'an that you may be in need of, individually or collectively, physically or spiritually. But you are in need of practicing.

No one can practice without a person to teach him how to practice. The *Shari'ah* is all the rules mentioned in the Holy Qur'an, and *tariqah* teaches people how to practice those rules. As a believer must learn the holy orders of Allah Almighty, so he needs someone to teach him practicing. Therefore Allah Almighty sent His beloved servant, Sayyidina Muhammad ﷺ to his people to teach them.

When he first met Gabriel ﷺ, then from the heavens there came on earth a golden throne, and angels took Sayyidina Muhammad ﷺ and made him sit on that throne. Then Gabriel touched the edge of his wing on earth. A spring came, and Gabriel made *wudu*, the Prophet ﷺ watching. Then Gabriel ﷺ told him to do the same washing, saying, "That is for you and your nation. Whoever does as you are doing, he will get clean from all sins, spiritually and physically clean."

Wudu is mentioned in the Holy Qur'an, but Gabriel came to show *how* to make *wudu*. We are in need to look and to practice. There are five hundred orders in the Holy Qur'an, mentioned by the Prophet ﷺ. He is the first explainer of the Holy Qur'an; for twenty-three years the Qur'an came from the heavens, but the meanings he had been given in his heart. All of his speech is an explanation of the Holy Qur'an. When he did something, that was *sunnah*,[3] or when he said something, or when he looked at the actions of his *sahabah* and did not object. Throughout the whole of his life, his sayings and actions were the practice of the meanings of the Holy Qur'an. The Qur'an came from Allah, but its meanings were given to his heart.

As the Prophet ﷺ taught his Companions how to practice, we are also in need. The *sahabah* were the teachers of all nations; everyone was in need of one of them to follow. Without following, it is so difficult to reach to real faith and worship.

Now people are understanding that learning is enough for practicing. But they are wrong, because the first order to the *sahabah* was to follow the Prophet ﷺ, making it *fard*, obligatory, as well as *sunnah* to follow him.

If you are not accepting to be a servant to anyone, how can you be a servant to your Lord? By serving someone, we may learn the manners of serving the Lord. There must be someone to destroy our ego, breaking its claims to be Lord and commander, to rule over us, because it never likes anyone to be over itself. The whole of the Qur'an and *hadith* are to make our ego to be more humble, as much as possible. Put it down as much as you can!

In books there may be written medicines for all diseases, but a physician must learn how to cure from *someone*. And as a first step, we need to prepare ourselves so that we may be able to carry orders.

I was with my Grandshaykh for forty years and still I am under his orders (if They cut off their divine help, we are going to be useless; with their divine support we may stand on our feet). And most of the *murids* who came to visit him were asking, "Any orders, O my master?"

He used to say, "O my son, you are free to choose. According to your inspirations, you are free." And he was saying to me, "If I am ordering, up

---

[3]In this text, *Sunnah* refers to the body of the Prophet's practices, while *sunnah* refers to an individual practice.

to now I don't see anyone to carry orders. It is too difficult for them. They can't carry such commands."

You are free. If two ways are coming, you may choose as you like. But the shaykh must have some powers. Even though *murids* may think they are choosing, he makes them to choose. It is freedom, because our ego likes to be free, but still he makes him go to that side.

That is for juniors, not seniors. But we don't like to be always juniors; we must improve, be able to carry orders. That is the reason that Allah covers our destiny, because if we knew our destiny, we would ask to escape. Therefore, by His mercy He orders us, "Choose this," so that people think they are free, and so they feel peace and satisfaction in themselves.

Among all people, saints have reached to the point of looking at their destiny and they are not afraid to go on to their destiny—as Sayyidina 'Ali⁴ ﷺ said to his murderer, who was his horse keeper, "*Ya qatili,* O my murderer!"

And his horse keeper said, "O my master, kill me so I may not kill you."

And 'Ali ﷺ said, "Oh, do you think I should do that and be *your* murderer? Without your doing anything to me, how could I kill you?" He knew and was not looking for any defense for himself, such as sending his murderer to another country; no, going on to his destiny.

The Prophet ﷺ kissed one of his grandsons, Sayyidina Husain ﷺ, on his mouth, and kissed the other on his neck. One was poisoned, one's head was cut off; *he knew.* And when the people of Iraq called Sayyidina Husain ﷺ [and promised] to support him,⁵ other *sahabah* cried and said, "*Ya sayyidi,* my master, don't go!" All of them cried but he said, "I must go," and he

---

⁴The Prophet's cousin and son-in-law, and the fourth of the rightly-guided caliphs.

⁵That is, when the Muslims of the Iraqi city of Kufa begged Sayyidina Husain ﷺ, the Prophet's grandson, to come to them and promised to support his claim to the caliphate.

went and fell on the beach of the Tigris as a martyr. They[6] are on the highest level of faith, to carry out the Will of Allah Almighty.

We are the lowest-standard believers, but still we are honored. Yet it is not enough to be on the lowest level. You must improve to real *iman*, faith, till there is clear to you your destiny. Therefore, we need someone, to obey his orders.

That is the way to reach that highest level of *iman*. If not obeying someone, it is impossible. All of Grandshaykh's Associations,[7] assemblies, during thirty or forty years, were in the same direction, to make attenders and followers to carry orders. And that is the ordinary standard of Islam; below that standard you can't call it Islam. Islam means to submit. If we not able to carry orders, there is only the name.

Now, as the Prophet 🕮 said for our time, there are people with only the name but no meaning of Islam. It is an order to follow a person, to be obedient to him, who can teach you to be obedient to all the orders of Allah, to prepare you for carrying orders.

Which thing prevents a person from preparinq himself to carry out orders? Ego says, "Don't be obedient to anyone except me!" And if you are following its commands, you are never going to be obedient to your Lord Almighty.

Tariqah makes you firstly to carry the commands of the *Shari'ah*,[8] the most basic level of Islam. When you are prepared, then comes the second step. The first step is on earth, the second in the Heavens. When you are firm on the first step, the second one takes you to the Heavens, because at the second step, you are going to be almost free from ego; at the second

---

[6]"They" refers to such saints and holy people, who, although knowing that a terrible end awaits them, nevertheless go toward it with total trust in the rightness of their Lord's decrees.

[7]*Sohbet* (from the Arabic suhbah, meaning companionship, friendship or association with someone), a conversation, talk or chat; in this context, the discourse of a shaykh.

[8]The canonical law of Islam, derived primarily from the Qur'an and the Prophet's *Sunnah* (practice).

step, you are prepared to accept and agree with the Will of Allah, with your destiny. When your *nafs*, your ego, is finished, you may enter the Heavens. But no one enters the Heavens by his ego; prohibited!

Every Association [of ours] is going to be from the Holy Qur'an or holy *Hadith* or Grandshaykh's sayings, to make you able to carry your destiny. You must be able and brave enough to walk towards it. Allah says, "If you are pleased with My Will, I am pleased with you." When you say, "As You like," He says, "O My servant, as *you* like, also." ▲

3: the need to turn to and follow a qiblah

May Allah Almighty give us good understanding of His holy verses in His Last Message, the Holy Qur'an.

He created man and He gave to everyone a heart. Our heart, He has made it for Himself; it belongs to the Lord Almighty. That is the most important part of man and the most precious; the spiritual power center is in the heart. The heart commands the body. It commands the mind, also.

And now people are claiming that the heart is under the command of the brain, but in reality control of the whole body comes through the heart. Don't think it is only a piece of flesh, like a fist. That is its physical shape, but in its place is a spiritual heart that controls the flesh heart and the whole body.

You know that everyone translates his feelings through his heart, not through his mind. And the real heart is always turning; according to the conditions that you are living in, it turns. And when it turns, you are going to appear in different conditions or states. It is impossible for a person to appear in the same state; always he is going to be changed. In Arabic, "*qalb*," heart, means "turned, changed." And when your heart is changed, your condition or your state is going to be changed.

Allah is the Creator and He knows well about our hearts. Like that lamp in mini-cab stations,[9] our heart quickly turns. But Allah made our hearts to be fixed in one direction, not to be lost.

---

[9]In England, minicab stations are recognizable by their revolving yellow lights.

You can't speak of a "direction" for Allah. He is in every direction, not in one only; He *created* directions. Men are in need to turn their faces to one direction. Therefore, when the first man came on earth, he asked to turn his face towards the Divine Presence. Then Allah sent to him a house from Paradise made of a red ruby, shining, lighted, and it landed at the place where the Holy Ka'bah was [later] built, because we need of turning to some direction to make our hearts fixed in that direction.

Adam was ordered to come to that palace, that Paradise-building of red ruby, and go around it and to pray towards it from four directions. Allah made for the first man a *qiblah*, to be a focus for his body and for his physical heart, to turn towards that direction.

It was the first *qiblah* for the first man. And we are saying, "If it is an empty building, there is no meaning in turning towards that Ka'bah." But we are asking for a *qiblah* in our real hearts. If you do not find that real Ka'bah but only that outwardly visible building, your heart will never gets a direction for reaching the Divine Presence. That *qiblah*, [our heart's *qiblah*], is in order to find a way to the Divine Presence.

That outwardly visible Ka'bah leads to the first level of the Seven Heavens, *Bait al-Ma'mur*.[10] (There is one *qiblah* in each heaven; then comes *Kursi*;[11] then comes *'Arsh*.[12]) And the first *qiblah* was the Ka'bah.

After the Ka'bah was built, Allah ordered the second *qiblah* to be in Quds, *Bait al-Maqdis*[13]—not Prophet David's ﷺ building, but, according to traditions, forty years after Abraham's ﷺ building,[14] there was the original *Bait al-Maqdis*. Therefore, for the Children of Isra'il, that *Bait al-Maqdis* was their *qiblah*. And for a while the Seal of the Prophets ﷺ was ordered to turn

---

[10]The spiritual prototype of the Ka'bah in the first heaven.

[11]The Divine Seat.

[12]The Divine Throne. These terms are to be understood as metaphors denoting Allah's endless greatness, glory, power, dominion and majesty.

[13]The Sacred House in Jerusalem, built on the spot where Solomon's Temple would later stand.

[14]That is, the K'abah, as mentioned in Bukhari, 4:636.

faces towards *Quds ash-Sharif.*[15] Then Allah made the Prophet ﷺ to turn towards the Holy Ka'bah.[16]

Bodies must turn towards that direction. But more than that *qiblah*, even, a person must have someone who represents the *qiblah* spiritually. At the time of the Prophet ﷺ, no one except himself represented the real Ka'bah; the real *qiblah* for the *sahabah* was *he*. Outwardly, the *sahabah's* praying was like our praying, but in reality theirs was quite different from our praying because they turned with their hearts to the Prophet ﷺ, who represented *Haqq*, Truth. That is the reason why, even if all *awliya*, saints, gathered together, it would be impossible to reach the level of the worshipping of even one *sahabi*, Companion of the Prophet ﷺ. Their worshipping was the most precious.

After the Prophet ﷺ, all the *sahabah* represented him, but the one who represented him best was Abu Bakr ؓ.[17] Therefore, the *sahabah* ran, even before burying Rasul-Allah ﷺ, to Abu Bakr ؓ to make *bayah*[18] and turn their hearts towards him, because someone must always represent Allah Almighty. There must be one *khalifah*, caliph, of Allah; everyone must be under that one's command, everything must move under his will power. And Abu Bakr ؓ was the *qiblah* for all the *sahabah*, the real one.

Then, over time, the *sahabah* went everywhere, and from among them, also, there were *qiblahs* for people. At every time, there must be one to represent the main *qiblah*. Then, from that one, there may be, in different places, by his spiritual powers, various people as *qiblahs*.

Allah Almighty orders mankind to turn towards the Holy Ka'bah physically, and He also asks us to turn towards the real *qiblah*, Sayyidina Muhammad ﷺ. And as long as they are not doing it, no peace, no agreement among nations; impossible.

---

[15]Jerusalem the Honored.

[16]Qur'an 2:142-150.

[17]The Prophet's father-in-law and close friend, who later became the first caliph of Islam.

[18]Pledge of commitment and loyalty.

So many people are here now. We are turning our faces towards *qiblah* and our hearts, through Muhammad 🌿, towards Allah Almighty. That gives us peace and mercy. If you are turning your faces towards Ka'bah behind the *imam*,[19] mercy comes pouring over people, and then divine love is sent and covers them.

Everyone is in need to find a real *qiblah* in his life. If not finding, even if he enters the Ka'bah, he may find nothing. He must find something around it and inside it. It is not empty.

We need to find and follow a *qiblah*, every time, and it should be a guide for us to heavenly Ka'bahs, towards the Divine Throne. What does it mean, "Throne," without Someone there? Without the Lord, what is the meaning of the Throne? And we are asking for *that* one.

Now, people, if they don't turn their faces towards the Ka'bah, their hearts are always turning and giving troubles; if not fixing to a Ka'bah, no peace and satisfaction. If looking, they may find some ones who represent the Lord, Almighty Allah, and their hearts are pouring blessings and divine love and mercy on you. ▲

---

[19] The leader of a congregational prayer.

4: about being a sincere servant to our lord

We are asking blessings from Allah Almighty, and we have been ordered to do everything for the pleasure of Allah.

It is impossible to do something for the pleasure of Allah Almighty if you are not sincere, the Seal of the Prophets ﷺ informed his nation fifteen centuries ago. Because who is a prophet? The one who informs about coming days and events, he is a prophet; if not knowing about coming days, he is an ordinary man. And saints must step in the footsteps of the Prophet ﷺ or they can't be saints. Prophets also can't be prophets if they can't follow in the steps which Almighty Allah appoints for them to step in.

All the *sahabah*, the Companions of Sayyidina Muhammad ﷺ, were following in the footsteps of the Prophet ﷺ; if not following, they could not be *sahabah*. The places where he put his feet must be well-known by *awliya*. Those places are lighted; everywhere in Hijaz where he put his blessed feet is lighted.

Once the son of Sayyidina 'Umar ؓ was journeying on the road to Mecca for pilgrimage. He arrived at a crossroad and left it, and went by the next one, turning. His friends said, "Oh! What is the reason?"

He said, "I saw our beloved Prophet ﷺ—he reached this point and turned. Therefore I like to follow his path."

He saw those lights and followed them; the one to whom Allah gives His lights, he may see and follow. But He never gives without sincerity. The Prophet ﷺ had *qadam as-sidq*, the steps of truthfulness. You can't step towards your Lord Almighty Allah's presence if you don't have steps of truthfulness. If you have that, you may reach.

Now, I was expecting for two days [to make] an Association, and I do not know except what They are making me to speak. I am asking my Lord's divine favors for everyone attending our Association. I don't like official things because if officiality comes, sincerity goes.

The Prophet ﷺ came on earth from the Divine Presence. Jesus Christ ﷺ went from the earth to the Heavens, but Muhammad—he was there and he was ordered to come to be with the people of the Lord.[20] He was the most sincere person, and he sat with slaves, women, children, with everyone, and quickly went to their level. He was the most humble of creatures, and he said, "I sit as slaves sit and I eat as slaves eat."

That is the top point of humbleness. He was not an official one. But he said, "When the Last Days approach, sincerity will be taken up and people will be official ones."

Among believers, sincerity is wanted more than anything else. But now 'religious' people are also official nothing remaining of religion except its name, and you can't find anything except official forms. Even Muslims are trying to make some associations with membership. But if officiality comes, sincerity goes.

When the Prophet ﷺ gave information about the truth, he said that what the People of the Book are doing, my nation is going to follow step by step. There should come a time for my nation when you will not find Islam except as a name, people practicing it officially.

There is an expression among Turkish Muslims; they say "man of religion" for an *imam* or a *muezzin*.[21] I am saying that they are putting every-

---

[20]Referring to the Holy Prophet's *Me'raj* or Night Journey to the Heavens , during which he was admitted to the utmost point of nearness to God Almighty among all created beings.

[21]In Turkey and many other Muslim countries, both the *imam* who leads the prayer and the *muezzin* who makes the call to prayer are government employees or officials.

thing onto them, paying them and resting; the others are free.[22] It is a bad expression; all believers are "men of religion." Why are *you* not going to be a servant of Allah? What rank is more honorable than being the servant of Allah?

Endless honors may be for certain people. Allah Almighty honored the Prophet 變 by giving him the biggest miracle, the Night Journey. When he returned in the morning time, he informed the people of Mecca about that journey-by-night and the unbelievers were astonished. Even the *sahabah* were too astonished. From Mecca to Jerusalem was forty days' journey by camel, but he claimed that during one night he had gone and come to Jerusalem, and after that to the Heavens and beyond the Heavens!

Believers must use their hearts for believing, not their minds. The famous caliph of the Muslims, one of the grand-*wazirs* of the Prophet 變 during his life-time, Sayyidina 'Umar 變, when heard this news [of the Prophet's *Me'raj*] from someone, he did not go to the Prophet 變 but he went to Sayyidina Abu Bakr 變, asking, "O Abu Bakr, did you hear about the miraculous news? What do you think?"

Abu Bakr 變 said, "O 'Umar, who is telling that news?"

"The Prophet of Allah."

He said, "Enough, O 'Umar! Even more than that I would believe." And he [Abu Bakr] is the father of the Naqshbandis.[23]

These words may be too big for scholars. They are thinking that their knowledge is the limit of knowledge and there is no more. And they are correct up to their limit, but after their limit, they must leave it to someone else. If Allah's lights enter into a heart, that heart gets wider and wider and wider.

---

[22]That is, under such a system, total responsibility for people's religion is placed on paid religious officials, while others see themselves as not having any responsibility.

[23]The chain *(silsilah)* of *awliya* and grandshaykhs of the Naqshbandi Tariqah originates with Sayyidina Abu Bakr 變, while all other *tariqahs* go back to Sayyidina 'Ali 變.

The Prophet ﷺ has 313 or more beautiful names and he has been honored. He has been honored unlimitedly because he was the representative of Allah Almighty, and, as we are saying, every Holy Name of Allah appears or manifests in the Prophet ﷺ and gives honor to him. And among all those names, he was very pleased when Allah described him in the Holy Qur'an as being His servant.[24]

He was so happy to be servant to such a Lord. And that is an honor for everyone. You must try! That is following the steps of Muhammad ﷺ—to be servants, sincere, humble servants. Think what an honor you have been given. Don't be 'official,' don't be a 'member'. Try to be a sincere servant to Almighty Allah.

This is our 'feast' today. It is enough to listen to these words from a humble one. May Allah accept you! ▲

---

[24] 2:23, 8:41, 17:1, 25:1, 53:10, 57:9, 72:19.

5: concerning the holy prophet's knowledge of the future and sayyidina mahdi

May Allah grant us inspirations through His beloved Sayyidina Muhammad 舉 and through His beloved *awliya*, saints.

The Prophet 舉 told everything about the future; he never left out anything. For twenty-three years he taught people the Qur'an and its meanings, and he made everything clear up to the Day of Resurrection, for this life and hereafter, for Paradise and Hells; *everything* he made clear. But now among scholars, there are some so-doubtful people, doubting everything, and they are trying to put the whole of the Prophet's 舉 sayings into forty *hadiths*.

There must be millions of *hadiths* over twenty-three years. He made clear the Holy Qur'an for all nations, up to the end; it was his duty to make clear this holy Book. How can you say there are only forty *hadith* and not accept others? They and Satan are equal. They are saying, "We only need the Qur'an, no need for anything else."

Allah says in the Holy Qur'an, "Accept everything that My Prophet says,"[25] but pride is preventing them. Sayyidina Muhammad 舉 is the most

---

[25]See 8:20, 24:62, 33:36 and many other verses of similar meaning. This is alluded to in the following ahadith:

I have indeed been given the Qur'an and something similar to it together with it, yet the time is near when a man reclining on his couch will say, "Just follow this Qur'an; what you find permissible in it, consider it permissible, and what you find prohibited in it, treat it as prohibited." But what Allah's Messenger has prohibited is like what Allah [Himself] has prohibited. (Abu Dawud and Ibn Majah)

true one; among mankind, no one can be more true than him. And he said, about our time, that all mankind are too proud (They are preventing me from speaking something wrong; my heart is in *Their* hands).

After the Prophet 🌸 was the period of caliphs. He said that the first period of his nation would be a period of caliphs, then the period of *'umara*, rulers, *'umara al-muminin*.[26] But there must be one *'amir*[27] for Muslims; if they do not make an *'amir* over themselves, to obey him, they are all sinners. There must be an *'amir* to implement the *Shari'ah*. But now everyone thinks *he* should be the *'amir*.

From the West wing, the power of Islam came up to France, near Paris. Then their period was finished and *muluk*, kings, came—the Ottoman *sultans*, and from the mother's side they reached back to the Prophet 🌸; the first *sultan's* wife was a *sayyid*.[28] And then kings came, up to Sultan 'Abdul-Hamid.[29]

In his time, there came a revolution which took him down from his throne. Then the fourth period came, the time of *jababirah*, tyrants. In every country, even when non-Muslim kings went, tyrants came, the king coming down and a Red one, a bad one, coming to destroy everything—so proud, throwing the Holy Qur'an from their hands. "Command is coming from my lips for life and death"; so many thousands of people killed in Turkey after the Revolution, and everywhere else!

There was Hajjaj ibn Yusuf, Hajjaj *adh-Dhalim*,[30] the well-known oppressor in Islam. Someone said, "O Hajjaj, you go back to the time of 'Umar and you have seen his justice. Why are you like this?"

Let me not find one of you reclining on his couch when he hears something that I have commanded or forbidden, saying, "I do not know. We followed [only] what we found in the Book of Allah." (Ahmad, Abu Dawud, Tirmidhi and Ibn Majah)

[26] Head of the believers, i.e., Muslims.

[27] Leader or head; the caliph was known as *'amir al-muminin*, the commander of the believers.

[28] A descendant of the Prophet 🌸.

[29] The last of the Ottoman rulers, deposed in 1908.

[30] Hajjaj the Tyrant.

He said, "Bring me the people of 'Umar and I may rule like him!"

Now it is the time of tyrants and dictators. Some characteristics of those dictators must be with ourselves, because they are taking their powers from the people. They are only like taps. If honey comes through pipes, honey comes; if vinegar comes, the taps give vinegar.

Everyone is proud now, no humble people; exceptions never change rules. And since "*naba'*" in Arabic means "news," every news that the Qur'an informed about must have an appointed time to appear.

The appointed time of dictators arrived from 1908; up to today it is seventy-nine years. I hope for it to be finished with eighty; I hope that a great revolution will come. The great French Revolution, which was also an opening for tyrants, putting the heads under the feet and the feet in the place of heads, was in 1789. After two years it will be two hundred years.

For every piece of news, there is an appointed time. Allah is the most practical One. Every news that is appointed just comes on time, not early, not delayed; it must appear at its appointed time. And He appointed a time for Sayyidina Mahdi ﷺ.[31]

The Prophet ﷺ informed all nations that after the four periods, after those tyrants, there should come a just one, supported by divine powers, to clean the whole earth from all tyrants. Only *he* can do this; for his honor there will come a *shari'ah*, for no one else. And he will not bring the *Shari'ah* that we are using now, he will bring a virgin *shari'ah*.

The Holy Qur'an is virgin; how could he reach that secret? But during the Night Journey, Allah gave it to Muhammad ﷺ in the Divine Presence.

Muhammad ﷺ is the greatest prophet, greater than anyone among heavenly beings, mankind and jinn. It is impossible for anyone to know the greatness of our Prophet ﷺ except his Lord. Gabriel is the Prophet's ser-

---

[31] The divinely-appointed leader whose coming during the End-Time of this world is foretold in many *hadiths*.

vant, not his teacher; his teacher is Allah. Only *he* reached to the Divine Presence, no other prophet.

When he went up, he saw Gabriel, lying like a carpet in his station out of divine *haybah*, awe of Allah's greatness and majesty. And Allah Almighty gave Muhammad 鷺 a trust in a safe; no one can imagine the glory of that trust. And He said to His Prophet 鷺, "Keep this till your fortieth grandson, Mahdi, comes. When he comes, you will open it for him." My Grandshaykh told me about that. Now, also, he is speaking.

When Mahdi comes. . . Now he is ready and Allah Almighty is keeping him in a safe place between Yemen and Hijaz. No one can approach; there is quicksand. His headquarters is protected. And now the Prophet 鷺 will give that trust to him.

When he comes and says "*Allahu akbar!*" that power of the secret of the Holy Qur'an will come like lightning all around the world and destroy all technology. When he gives *takbir*,[32] all that news must come to pass. *Tuba*, happiness and pleasure, for those people who will reach to those days! All proud ones will be taken away. Ask to be humble servants to that beloved one.

Only Grandshaykh has permission to speak about such things. No one else in the East and West may speak. ▲

---

[32]Saying "*Allahu Akbar*, God is the Most Great."

6: following the ways of holy men

May Allah Almighty bless you during this holy month; you are coming here and listening. I am seeing that our assembly is not an ordinary assembly or association. This is not an official meeting and we are not official people and attenders. We are carrying responsibility only towards Allah Almighty.[33]

If a person carries responsibility towards his Lord, he tries to do his best. And we are trying to do our best for each one of mankind living on earth. We are asking happiness and pleasure and peace for everyone, here and Hereafter; we are trying to give as much benefit as possible to everyone. That is the main aim of the holy people who lived before and who are living now and who will live after our time.

This life began with a holy one, Sayyidina Adam, and since his time there have been, at every time, holy ones, never absent. They are only living for others, not for themselves. They are sacrificing themselves for mankind, and therefore Allah Almighty rewards them in Paradise like no one else.

We are trying to follow the ways of holy men. We must try to be holy ones because they are *real* believers; they *really* believe in Allah Almighty and the Day of Resurrection, *really* believe in Paradise and Hells. We must follow their ways and try to reach high standards of belief—not only by talking, but we must show our belief through our bodies' activities and actions because believers show that they believe through their actions. Actions are evidences of holy people, and we are trying to reach their standard, the highest station of mankind.

---

[33]That is, not to any government, institution or organization.

Some people in our times are carrying the title of "holiness" but they are empty ones. We must try to be *real* holy ones so that it should be said for us in the Divine Presence, "Your Holiness." Prophets and their real successors, *awliya*, are holy ones, and you can't be holy without reaching one of those holy ones. You must try to find one.

They are not found easily. Like diamonds and precious stones, they are difficult to find. Among people, holy ones will be up to the end of this world, but don't be cheated by empty titles, official titles. Try to find real ones, whose names are written on heavenly stations. If anyone reaches such people, those holy ones also cover those who reach them.

But they do not come easily into your hands. They make so many examinations for that person, so many times trying him. And sometimes they are showing some perfection[34] and people are running after them.

Abu Yazid Bistami was always traveling to get in touch with people as much as possible; They always want to transfer their spiritual lights to others. Firstly, all prophets were travelers, to get in touch with more people. Whether accepting them or not doesn't matter; they have some powers, passing from their hearts to people. Impossible for a person to meet a prophet without being affected. As radiation comes on animals or plants or people but does not quickly appear, their hearts are most important for giving their lights to people. Even at the last, those people should be affected.

Awliya, saints, are also following the same ways and they also travel. In Abu Yazid's time there were no passports, no customs, no borders; from East to West one could go. He was coming and showing his miraculous powers, and people, like bees coming on honey, were gathering around him.

He gave something to them and some of them were going with him (all of them were attracted but only some of them were suitable to be with him). As we know, Allah Almighty has made for everyone a private position, to be there;[35] if everyone left his job and came [to be with a *wali*], no

---

[34]*Karamat*, the miracles of *awliya*.

[35]That is, each individual's particularl life situation and conditions.

more would life continue as Allah wants it to continue. Everyone must keep his position and [at the same time] must keep his spiritual relationship with that holy one, and he can reach billions. That one's spiritual powers may cover the whole universe, because the whole universe without that holy one is cheap but with that one it is precious.

As we have been invited to visit the Ka'bah, we are in need to find a holy servant of the Lord. The Ka'bah must be visited once in a lifetime at least, and also that holy one who represents the Prophet 🌺 must be known and visited, even once in a lifetime, because the Holy Ka'bah stands by that one.

That is *Sultan al-Awliya*.[36] He is that one who gives holiness to the servants of the Lord, Almighty Allah. He may be represented among 124,000 holy ones at any time.[37] They represent that holy one who represents the Seal of the Prophets 🌺, by whom the Holy Ka'bah stands.

I am asking pilgrims, "What did you see at the Holy Ka'bah? Did you meet any holy one?" But no one is asking to meet anyone. For what are you going—*only to see that building?* You must look for that one who represents the Holy Prophet 🌺. But now believers are official ones, all of them. If real ones, at the first step they may ask permission to enter from the boundaries of those holy places, and whoever enters with full *adab*[38] meets the guardians of those places, holy guardians.

Full *adab* to the holy places is to come and say, "I have left everything that my heart is occupied with of this life." If They [the holy guardians] see that your heart is for your Lord only, They may welcome you, but if you have come to acquire the title of "*Hajji*,"[39] they may say, "Go away!" If you came for the sake of your Lord, They see your heart and They welcome you from the beginning. Even the Holy Ka'bah may come to welcome you, as

---

[36]The highest ranking saint among *awliya*, the greatest grandshaykh.

[37]As there have been 124,000 prophets since the time of Adam 🌺, there are at all times 124,000 *awliya* on earth.

[38]Correct manners.

[39]One who has performed the pilgrimage (*Hajj*).

it came to Rabi'at al-Adawiyah.[40]   She was a descendant of the Prophet, Sayyidina Muhammad ﷺ, a lady, but she reached a level that only few men have reached.

If ladies are asking for physical equality, there is never going to be [physical] equality. If equal, there must be all men or all women. Men and women are never going to be equal; there must be something wrong if they are asking to be the other sex. And they are asking but they are wrong.

Spiritually there is equality. Women have more ability to reach the Divine Presence, and also, among spiritual beings, women have been given something else through their spiritual life's high standards.   Men are also equal, but their spiritual appearance, manifestation, is of another kind. Both of them have been honored by Allah Almighty; no one knows the limits of that honor. That discussion is nonsense, the lowest rubbish. If you [women] are feeling oppressed, don't go and work! Leave them [men] to do it; you sit in your houses!

I just took this from Rabi'at al-Adawiyah; she will be happy if we accept it. She went to pilgrimage at the time of Hasan al-Basri. He arrived at the Holy Ka'bah and saw the Ka'bah only as a shape, standing, leaving only a shadow, but the Ka'abah itself was not there. He asked, "O my Lord, where is Your Holy House?"

The answer came by 'Telephone":[41]   "Rabi'ah is coming and the Ka'abah has gone to welcome her."

She was at 'Arafat, the holy mountain.[42] That day she was useless for praying[43] and she was crying (women think that something is wrong for them not to pray at that time, but it is a grant from Allah to them, carrying

---

[40]Rabi'a Basri.

[41]*Hatif ar-Rabbani*, the divine Voice, by which some of Allah's chosen servants are sometimes addressed.

[42]The mountain in whose vicinity pilgrims assemble during the *Hajj* to supplicate and ask for Allah's forgiveness.

[43]That is, due to menstruation, she was unable to observe *salat*, prayers.

some burden). She cried, and Allah, by *hatif ar-rabbani*, said to all the pilgrims, "This year your pilgrimage was not acceptable, but, because of her crying, all of you are accepted!"

We must look after ourselves. When Abu Yazid showed some perfection, people ran after him. Sometimes he tried some of them by showing something that no one would accept. Then they left him and went away, and he left, also.

They [*awliya*] may try you by several ways. If you do not change [due to their tests], they may accept you, because it is not easy to follow. Therefore they are choosing the one who should be with them always. Even once a year, you need to see them, giving you new power and taking away burdens. ▲

7: the greatness of divine mercy in the face of our sins

We, all of us, belong to mankind, and each one is like a leaf on a big tree, the tree of mankind.

It is mentioned in traditions that there is a big tree in the Heavens. On that tree there are leaves, of the number of mankind from the beginning up to the end, so many leaves, and on each one is written the name of one of mankind.

Forty days before a person dies, his leaf dies, and on the day of his death it falls down in front of 'Azra'il 峚, the Angel of Death, and he sees who that person is and takes his soul. Sometimes our ears may ring. There is a tradition that when someone's leaf comes down, it may touch some others. If touching your leaf, your ear rings, and you say, *"Inna lil-Lahi wa inna ilayhi raj'iun."*[44]

Each person is an individual, never going to be like another one. You can't be the same as another one; each one must be distinctive, must be unique, in his personality. Even twins must be different, also. They may be so similar in their forms but it is impossible to be similar in their characteristics.

That shows the Lord's endless Will Oceans and endless Power and Wisdom and Knowledge and Artistry Oceans. We may find among mankind some similar characteristics; there may be some people on the same

---

[44]"Indeed, we belong to Allah, and indeed we shall return to Him." (2:156)

lines, but everyone, in his characteristics, manifests a special personality among people in the Divine Presence. And Allah Almighty, the Lord of mankind, knows with absolute knowledge about everyone's characteristics and everyone's attributes. He is the only One who is able to gather all of them, in spite of their differences, to make them to meet on the same point, and He is able to send His Message so that it should be interesting to everyone from some direction.

Therefore, we have the Holy Qur'an, a one-volume book of about six hundred pages, 6,666 verses and 114 *surahs*.[45] In that limited size, the Lord, Almighty Allah, is giving to everyone, according to their attributes, suitable examples or guidance or anything that they may need. In the Holy Qur'an, you may freely reach your private destination; without getting into a confined space, you may find your way through the Holy Qur'an to your destination.

Its size is so small but it contains, for all mankind, their private destinations. It is a grant from Allah Almighty to His servants, to make them reach their destinations and endless honors in the Divine Presence. And everyone's destination ends in the Divine Presence; no one's destination is *not* in the Divine Presence.

There is the holy *hadith*,[46] "*Sabaqat rahmati 'ala ghadabi*, My mercy outdoes My anger." That is a very, very, very great good tidings for rebellious ones: the Lord Almighty may be angry with His disobedient people, but even though He is able to punish them, finally His mercy comes and saves them. That is one of the greatest good tidings among the traditions which the Seal of the Prophets 🏵 has brought us.

Once a person came to the Prophet 🏵. (I heard this from my Grand-shaykh, to make more clear to you the wideness of divine Mercy Oceans. No matter how disobedient we may be, following our egos and Satan, Al-

---

[45]Chapters.

[46]That is, a *hadith qudsi*, in which Allah Most High speaks about Himself through the Prophet's tongue.

lah's Mercy Oceans are wider.) He came to the Prophet ﷺ and asked, "O Muhammad, do you think that Allah may forgive me?"

The Prophet ﷺ said, "What do you think about your sins?"

He said, "I am a very great sinner because I was an ignorant one, and I am asking now if it is possible to be granted forgiveness."

The Prophet ﷺ asked, "Your sins are more than mountains?"

"Yes."

"Bigger than all the oceans?"

"I think so."

"Are they bigger than the seven earths and seven heavens?"

"I think so. Bigger!"

"Are they bigger than the Divine Throne?"

"I think so."

Then the Prophet ﷺ stopped; up to that limit he could use his authority for intercession. And at that time Allah sent His archangel Gabriel, saying to tell what he had done. "He must tell his sins to you, and We have forgiveness for everyone. No matter how big his sins may be, they are never going to be bigger than Mercy Oceans. Let him tell those sins!"

He said, "O Muhammad, I was a king in my territory before Islam came, in the Time of Ignorance, and I was so proud. I had forty daughters and I never accepted to marry any of my daughters to anyone. Therefore, I myself married all of them. Then, when each one gave birth to a child, each one I killed and threw away."

The Prophet ﷺ stopped. And Allah Almighty said, "Even though he did that, he is repenting and unhappy, and his sins are burning him now. Even though he did that, I forgive him. He may continue towards his destination to reach to My Divine Presence. No one must cut off his hope of My Mercy Oceans!"

Allah does *such* things! Everyone has an ego, and ego always orders bad things; the worst things it always orders, and if it finds an opportunity, it may do *that*. During the Night Journey, Allah said, "O Muhammad, if I gave such a chance to My servants as I gave to Pharoah, all of them would be such a person!"

We must ask forgiveness. In our Naqshbandi Order we have a practice: asking forgiveness between one hundred to five hundred times for every sin we have done up to this day; and one hundred to five hundred times "*Astaghfirullah*,"[47] asking for protection from being left in the hands of our ego: "O my Lord, don't give any chance to my ego to do a sin." We are in need of that. Very important!

Some *awliya* were saying, "I am not afraid for past sins but I am afraid for the rest of my life, how it is going to be passed." Like this, like that, we have reached up to today and we can say "*Astaghfirullah*." But maybe after this time, up to the end, there may come a change in our life, to forget to make *sajdah*[48] or to forget to say "*Astaghfirullah*." No one can give you insurance against such a life.

This way gives an insurance: to ask, "O my Lord, don't give me a chance to be disobedient; don't leave me in the hands of my ego for even one moment." The Prophet ﷺ was praying, "O my Lord, don't leave me and my nation, my *ummah*, in the hands of our egos." One hundred to five hundred for past days, and up to five hundred for divine 'insurance,' and we hope that Allah never leaves us in the hands of our egos or of satans. ▲

---

[47]"I ask Allah's forgiveness."
[48]Prostration.

8: the meaning of *tariqah*: patience

We are in need of more *uns*, familiarity. It is important, and familiarity grows with people when their *iman*, faith, gets stronger.

Faith needs something to make it stronger, needs feeding. If you don't feed your faith, how is it going to be stronger? How—by eating more? We are eating too much but it is not getting to be stronger, getting fat physically but coming down spiritually. Therefore we must know what can feed our faith.

Eating and drinking are useless, perhaps making it weaker. *Fasting* makes it stronger. But we are looking for another thing that the Prophet ﷺ informed us about, and he informed us about everything that we need.

Once he was asked, "What is faith?"

He answered, "*As-sabr*, patience."

Iman means patience; they are equal. In one with whom there may be patience, *iman* may be with him. According to his patience, his *iman* grows and gets stronger.

The most important thing we need in this life is patience. Patience supports us physically and spiritually. Abu Yazid Bistami, *qaddas Allahu sirruhu*,[49] was asked, "What is the meaning of a person's being in *tariqah*? What is *tariqah* asking from us?"

He said, "To be patient with difficulties, with unliked actions or things."

---

[49]"May Allah sanctify his secret," the traditional invocation for *awliya*.

Everything may be unliked, distasteful, and we may find those kinds of distasteful things among people. Particularly in our time, there should be found too many distasteful actions among people.

At the beginning of the twentieth century, people were mostly keeping their old manners. Religious manners they were keeping, good manners among families, neighbors, among children; they were under the control of their religious rules. But day by day people's relationship to their good manners is getting weaker and weaker, and now it is just finishing. The reason is unlimited freedom, coming at the beginning of this century, and good manners are going away from families and people.

Freedom is making people, everyone, to do as they like, and so many disliked actions are appearing, now full-up. But we, as believers, have been asked to carry people; even with their bad manners, we have been asked to carry them. That means to be patient with people, and it gives strength to our faith.

The highest attribute for a person is to try to reach the attribute of Almighty Allah, patience. I heard from my Grandshaykh that every period of mankind is divided into ninety-nine divine appearances, manifestations. From the beginning of Sayyidina Adam up to today, there are manifestations of His ninety-nine Holy Names, and today His manifestation is *as-Sabur*, the Patient.[50]

Allah sees everything that His servants are doing, and He made the last Holy Name to be *as-Sabur*, the Most Patient One with His servants, never quickly angry. He is patient, and He made that Holy Name for governing the divine manifestation of patience for our time. If not, He would have quickly destroyed all the world now.

In past times, only a few people among most of our peoples were wrong ones, and there were whole nations which were destroyed and vanished because of a few of them. Now there are billions, and Allah is still carrying His servants. He is looking at what we are doing to Him and to

---

[50]*As-Sabur* is the ninety-ninth of the ninety-nine Holy Names of Allah.

each other, and as He is patient, most patient, endlessly patient, we, as His servants, must try to reach that attribute of Allah A1mighty. ▲

9: ðoıng everythıng for the sake of allah almıghty

Grandshaykh Shah Naqshiband was, and is, the main pillar of the Naqshbandi Order. If he were not in our chain, this *tariqah* would not have come into existence.

We are claiming to be in Their *tariqah*. His *khalifah*, deputy, Shaykh 'Alauddin al-Bukhari, was asking, "O my master, how can we know if a person belongs to the Most Distinguished Naqshbandi Order?"

He answered, "If a person is among a group of people with a Naqshbandi shaykh and he feels happy and pleased, that is enough sign that he belongs to this Order." It is a good sign for anyone who comes to our Association and feels peace and pleasure.

Important is to believe. Through your beliefs you may improve in heavenly ranks and stations. Unbelievers are preventing themselves from reaching heavenly stations by unbelief, but believers may reach station after station through believing.

We have, among traditions, descriptions of believers. There are some special prayers or fastings or readings of *dhikr* and so many actions which have reached us. They are precious and acceptable in the Divine Presence, and Allah is recording.

But in our times, believers are becoming sick, their beliefs becoming weak. Sickness is coming through our egos.

Our egos represent absolute laziness. You can't find any creature more lazy than our ego. If a person believes in some good actions, our egos are rejecting it and saying, "For what is that?" For a scholar, also, saying, "From where do you get this—from the Holy Qur'an or *hadith*?" If it is from *hadith*, trying to escape. If you ask an ostrich if it is a bird, it says, "I am a camel"; if you want to load it, it says, "No, I am a bird"; if you say, "Fly," it says, "No, I am a camel!"

Our egos, also—if you want them to do something, they always want to escape because they represent laziness. And we are just created to be the servants to our Lord, Almighty Allah, and a real servant asks to do, at every opportunity, more praying, fasting, reciting, making *dhikr, salawat*[51]; he is happy to do more and more. But in our time, people are under their egos' commands and they are asking, "From where are you taking those *dhikrs* and prayers?" And people are also jealous and want to prevent others from doing those precious worshippings.

Allah wants reasons for giving from His favors. Everyone who works for Allah, to make Him pleased, should be rewarded on the Day of Resurrection. And if a person hears about some good worship and does it, even if it is not mentioned in *hadith*, Allah should reward that person on Judgment Day as if he had acted according to *hadith*.

Allah Almighty is asking from His servants to occupy themselves more and more with His worship. *Any action that is done for Allah's pleasure is worship.* And we are asked to give more time for the sake of Allah.

Daily, for eight hours, you may be for your Lord, and you may do more than this, also. But Grandshaykh says those eight hours are not only for praying.

This meeting is for Allah Almighty. Our egos are not happy to be here, asking to go around London. And you are coming from Germany, from America, from Italy and Spain, from East and West; you are intending to come during Ramadan for the pleasure of Allah. From the time of your leaving home, all twenty-four hours, every day, are written for you as acting for Allah Almighty. Londoners, also; you are at work but your hearts are related or connected; all day you are thinking of being with the shaykh, with

---

[51]Invocation of blessings on the Holy Prophet ﷺ.

his Association. You are asking to be with this fortunate group of people, and for you, also, your names are written for the whole of Ramadan at your Lord's service.

With our intention, we may make our whole life for Allah. To live for Allah and to die for Allah—that is real servanthood. You are eating, drinking, sleeping, but it is for the sake of Allah, to make your Lord happy, not for your ego. And when He is pleased with you, He will make you pleased with Him. That is the highest happiness for a servant.

Your ego is asking to be even more free from every responsibility, but you are forcing it to be a sincere servant. Allah rewards that; our time's, our day's 'payment' for believers is excellent! For keeping a *sunnah*, He gives the reward of one hundred martyrs, and for obligatory worships and actions, the Prophet 🕮 kept back from saying that payment, Allah just hiding it. You should be very happy when you are given your rewards on the Day of Resurrection!

And also we are reaching that through praying and worshipping in our hearts, and this holy month is a very good opportunity for putting our hearts in the Divine Presence. We must always put our heart in His Divine Presence, a big opportunity for practicing so that we may put our face towards *qiblah* and our real face towards Allah, our physical face towards Ka'bah and real face towards Allah Almighty.

It is easy during Holy Ramadan. During nighttimes, after midnight, you may be with your Lord. *Even for five minutes, try to be with Him.* It should continue also after Ramadan; He is asking you to be with Him. He is with us, but we are not feeling or not trying to feel that He is in us. He is with ourselves, outside and inside. Even for some minutes, try to remember that.

He *must* be with you. If He takes away His power, you are going to be nothing. And that divine *sirr*, secret, is with *awliya*, also. They may be with you, also, inside and outside; remember that they may be with you. Grandshaykh must be with you, outwardly and inwardly; otherwise, you can't establish your station without them. During this holy month, it is easy when you are with your grandshaykh.

Be careful on that point: try to occupy yourself more all the time with Allah and His service; try to do everything for the sake of Allah and His Sayyidina Muhammad ﷺ—for His honor. If you do something for your family, make them happy for the sake of Allah. And wives may make their husbands happy for the sake of Allah, and it should be easy, not cutting their relationship. In everything, you may do your best for everyone, to make everyone happy for the sake of Allah, and they should be happy—and you, also. ▲

10: STRIVING FOR PERFECTION

May Allah Almighty grant all of us good understanding. Important is not to speak, but important is to listen and to understand correctly, not wrongly.

If a person listens with his heart, he may understand, but if he occupies his heart with something else, it is difficult to understand; he may *misunderstand*. It is not easy if a person misunderstands; he may do everything upside-down, feet in the place of head, abnormal. Therefore, give your attention. As you give, you are taking.

Allah Almighty is the Creator. And now in our time, there are two views, two ways of looking at the universe and its existence, two doctrines concerning this universe and everything in it. One group believes, and the other group thinks, "It is a reality that there is a universe in existence. But how did this universe come into existence—by itself or by Someone Else?"

Believers believe that this universe and everything existing has been brought into existence by Someone Else, and atheists say that it exists by itself. There is no other view. But if you look at both sides, anyone who has anything of knowledge or intelligence or wisdoms never says that this universe has been formed by itself. It is only the imagination of some people that it has been formed by itself. Wisdom and science and intellect deny that view, because every creature is in need of a creator.

If we look at the universe, we are so many creatures. Who can say that I am my own creator or that I can create? There are gigantic stars but yet they are fire. But fire destroys, burns, making everything vanish, and you can't imagine that fire brings anything into existence.

Physically we are not worth mentioning in the universe; an electron microscope in this universe can't even see you. You can see atoms? No! We, also, in this universe, have such a small position. But we are mighty creatures in the universe. In the universe, which one is perfect? *You, mankind, the perfect one!*

You may look with your eyes deeply into space. How is it possible? To the extent that we are mighty, Someone gives that *hiba*, gift, to us. So many kinds of animals are living, but who put that crown on you to be the king on earth, so that everything is under your command?

How are you denying it and saying that the universe can be by itself? Atheist people, either they are drunk or they are no-mind people. But it is such a dirty illness! Like rabies, that wrong view has quickly come, from one scholar to another. What is wrong with saying that an endlessly Powerful, endlessly Knowing One, endlessly Wise One, endlessly Willing One, endlessly Beautiful One, endlessly Powerful One created this universe, instead of saying that it is created by itself?

They are laughing at believing ones, saying, "There is no Creator." But mostly people are losing their intellect, so drunk. What is wrong with accepting a Most Merciful Lord for the entire universe? But they are devils, they are the servants of devils, asking to fight against good things!

And the Creator, "Allah" is His Name, His most important and greatest Name. His specific and proper Name is "Allah." "God" is not His name; "God" is only "*ilah*," deity. You are saying "*Theos*" or "*Dieu*" or "*Deo*," but they are not His proper name; even if you write it with a capital letter, it doesn't mean proper. In holy books, He is mentioned as "Allah."

He Almighty sent His prophets to mankind, from the first one up to the last. The divine attribute of the Lord Almighty is that He loves good ones and hates bad ones, and all the prophets who were sent to mankind, their attributes were also the same. All the prophets represent good ones, and everyone following them is a good one. Whoever goes against them, they are bad ones.

The last, the Seal of the Prophets ﷺ, his attribute, also, was that he advised people to be good ones and to love good ones. His nation's attribute is to love good ones and to be good ones, and to be against evil and devils[52] because they are enemies of mankind, of creatures, of prophets, of Allah Almighty. And we need to be trained in that attribute.

But you must have tolerance. Now it is impossible, except for prophets, to be one hundred per cent good ones—impossible, but fifty per cent, forty per cent, thirty per cent, sixty per cent you may approach. But you can't be absolute; even one per cent, if you can find it. And if you have more than one per cent, you must be tolerant of those people who have less than you. If you can find even one per cent, hold on to that one; he may improve, may be two or three per cent.

We are asking for perfection; we are not asking for animal life, with eating and drinking and sex only. You are created for perfection. Everything in this world was created for one purpose: for your perfection; everything is helping you to perfection. Therefore, we must try to improve. *Don't stand still!* Try to climb up the perfection-ladder, try to approach. Everything will help you.

If you do not reach one hundred per cent, you will be dealt with in the last moment of your life. If still not reaching, the grave will grind you and make you dust, to bring out a new form for you with perfection. If not enough, on the Day of Resurrection you should be dealt with by another dealing. If still not enough, after Resurrection you should be dealt with in Hells for perfection. ▲

---

[52]Meaning evil ones from among humankind and jinn.

11: taking away the veils from our hearts

May Allah grant us, through the Seal of the Prophets ﷺ, good understanding of the Holy Qur'an and holy *hadith* and the holy words of *awliya*.

Man is created and honored to be Allah's deputy in the universe, and Allah is addressing him. It is endless honor for mankind, that Allah, the Lord of the universes, is addressing them. The Greatest; He was the Greatest and He is and will be from pre-eternity to eternity.

We are nothing. Physically we are such small ones. But Allah made us something, addressing us, "O mankind, O My servants."

No one can imagine the honor of being addressed by the Lord of the universes. Don't think that you are His servants only during this short life. Were you nothing before this life?

There is a beginning for mankind, and their beginning only their Creator knows. All mankind were in the Divine Presence before coming to this temporary life. Have you thought, when we were in the Divine Presence, what our position was? Nothing? *To be servant to the Lord!*

We were and we are eternal servants. From pre-eternity up to eternity, we are His servants, only our servanthood in the Divine Presence was sincere and perfect. But Allah, in His wisdoms, wanted to give His servants more honor. He gave us *nur*, lights, and then He wanted us to have *nurun 'ala nur*,[53] to give us more light.

---

[53]"Light upon light." (24:35)

Allah dresses our souls in a physical body, giving us an ego that represents our physical body. And during our short life, Allah grants us also another light, from pre-eternity up to coming into this life—the light of His Holy Name, *ar-Rahman*.[54] That belongs to Mercy Oceans, that belongs to pre-eternity, reaching another Mercy Ocean from *ar-Rahim*,[55] belonging to Mercy Oceans, facing eternity.

We have been created between huge Mercy Oceans, and both of them have been granted to mankind. Therefore, Allah wants us to ask for more and more from those Mercy Oceans of *ar-Rahman, ar-Rahim*.[56] Do you think that His Mercy Oceans are within limits? *Don't think so!* Unlimited greatness and glory to our Lord, Allah Almighty!

Mankind on this planet, theyey are not only this limited number of human beings. When the Prophet 🌸 was on his Night Journey with Gabriel in the Seven Heavens, the Prophet 🌸 was standing, and beside him the archangel Gabriel was standing. And there was a parade, Sayyidina Muhammad 🌸 looking, of some of Allah Almighty's armies. Like lines, straight lines, they rode on horses, quickly passing and saluting the Prophet 🌸.

He looked but he did not find an end or a beginning for them. He asked about those armies and Gabriel said, "O beloved one of our Lord, I was created and was looking at their formations, and I never saw an end or a beginning."

Then the divine addressing came, saying, "No one can know the number of your Lord Almighty's armies." No limits for His armies or servants from among angels or among mankind!

Who was the first Adam and who will be the last one? Don't ask; your Lord knows! You are fortunate that you have been created among the chil-

---

[54]The Beneficent, Compassionate.

[55]The Merciful, the Mercy-Giving.

[56]Together, these two attributes of Allah Almighty denote infinite compassion, beneficence and mercy.

dren of Adams. Our Adam represents 124,000 Adams among the endless territories of our Lord, Almighty Allah.

Everything that belongs to our Lord, Almighty Allah, must be endless. He is the Creator and creation has been going on from pre-eternity up to eternity. If it were going to finish, Allah would finish. *Hasha*—never! He is the Lord of Creation, He may create in a second's time.

Scientists now are speaking about a 'big bang.' They are saying that in part of the trillionth part of a second, the universe appeared. That is their imagination. In less and even less than that part, Allah is creating. Now, also, huge universes are created, like this one, as they are imagining, in the trillionth part of a second.

He does not create empty universes but ones full of servants. It is impossible to imagine His greatness; He has endless greatness and endless Power Oceans! You can't find a unit of time without creation. You are only one of that huge creation's caravans, a very small one on a very small planet. But Allah honored you and gave you to understand big things so that we may understand something about His greatness.

We are candidates to know more and to reach divine Knowledge and Wisdom Oceans. Prepare yourself for that Divine Presence! That is the main goal of prophets with messages: *to prepare people for the Divine Presence.*

Our real beings have never moved from that Divine Presence. To where should they want to move, how *would* they move from the Divine Presence? Our real beings are in the Divine Presence, in endless, divine Light Oceans, and they are happy. From that real existence, only one ray comes into our physical bodies, and it is important for mankind to be here to carry that burden.

This physical body is a heavy burden on our real beings. But divine wisdoms give us more lights and we may take perfection during this short life, and that gives us more honor in the Divine Presence.

You can't judge concerning your being, here or there. Everyone is appointed to an important position during this life; everyone is put into an orbit towards his destination, and everyone's destination should end in the

Divine Presence. And Allah's addressing is for all mankind; Allah's absolute addressing is without difference between believers and unbelievers. He honored us before our coming here.

He is asking from His servants, in this life, to know and to open the veils from mankind, to look into pre-eternity at their *real* beings. Therefore, He sent prophets, to take the veils from their hearts. If you can follow their ways, those veils will be taken from you.

The day that those veils are taken away, there should appear to you some worlds and views and universes that never appeared before. If not, it is going to open to you when you leave this life for the eternal life. Mankind *must* reach the Divine Presence here or Hereafter, but it is the most honor if they reach it during this short life. Through Allah's messengers, we are asked to try to reach that Divine Presence during our life.

That is the summary of mankind and of existence. Today They granted us brief wisdoms to understand that you are the greatest one among creatures. You must know that, and you must try to be a humble servant to that One who granted you the greatest honor.

My Allah bless you and forgive us. Beyond these limits, there are unlimited wisdoms. I hope we will reach to Sayyidina Mahdi (A). Whoever can reach to his light-filled time, they may understand more and more.

We hope to be among his humble servants. His time is approaching, day by day. I see that that distance is going to be one or two or at most three years. At the longest, there are not more than three years; must be. He knows best.

That whole time will be lighted from this darkness. Nights will be lighter than sunny days; people will wait for nighttime to come quickly. Now, when night comes, some load comes on our hearts, but at that time, people will wait for nighttime because miraculous divine lights will appear in unimaginable, unknown colors. People at that time will fly through the earth and skies like angels by the power of their *dhikr*, no need for wings.

We are expecting to reach that time. But, O my Lord's servants, you must try to prepare yourselves with pure hearts. ▲

12: the importance of agreeing with allah's will

The Lord of the Universes, His attribute is to gather people, and, according to His Divine Will, all things are running to their destiny. It is important for everyone who is asking to be happy in this and the eternal life to know that everything, every event, happens by the Divine Will, divine rules. Nothing is going to be as everyone wants it to be.

Allah sent, through His messengers, several messages to inform people that there is Someone beyond your vision, knowledge, mind, imagination. Don't be a foolish one who thinks that there is only something that can be touched and seen, nothing beyond our vision. That is the ultimate ignorance imaginable!

It is mentioned in all traditions that the first man was Adam; in every message from the Lord of the heavens, we have been informed that that was Adam, the first man. But about two hundred years ago, someone spoke in the name of science (which is *not* science) and said that mankind has come from apes (maybe only that one came from apes). But every kind of creature must reproduce from its own kind; according to rules, inscribed by divine inscription, each one must bring forth the same kind of creature.

That first man, Adam, informed his children, "O my children, this universe is not only what you can see and touch." Beyond enormous distances, or closer than our looking, there may be huge universes.

Thousands and thousands of prophets were in touch with the unseen worlds that we call the Heavens and they were informing people. "You must believe that beyond that universe is Someone, and it is impossible for there to be two or three or four. Must be only *One*."

We are looking at the universes and seeing only One's Will and One's rules commanding and arranging everything. If there were more than One, one might say for fire not to burn and another might say to burn. We can't see two wills in one thing at the same time, and that is evidence that there is only One's Will.

Those who are looking at space, at stars and galaxies, astronomers, say that millions of galaxies are, all of them, moving in the same direction. None goes against it; all of them, like a river, are running towards the same direction, some quickly, some slowly. That is a great evidence that One beyond those galaxies is ordering them to run. Do they have motors or machines pushing them? Here, they are saying 'Nature.' Is there 'Nature' *there*, also?

You can look at trees in summer. Two or three months earlier, all trees were dry wood. Who gave them all the order to be green at the same time, none delayed? We must believe and know with certainty that there is One Will commanding everything; impossible for there to be anything contrary to that One's Will.

The most perfect ones among creatures are mankind. Allah Almighty authorizes us to do things and gives us free will, but that is also controlled by the absolute Will of the Creator. Don't be cheated and think you can do everything. His Will is controlling our will. He gave us free will for simple things, but don't think that your will affects your destiny. Your destiny is according to His Divine Will; you can't do anything.

And you must not be like a person who has been given a power and then claims to be the Lord of mankind, like Nimrod and Pharaoh. They were given power and then they said, "Oh, we are powerful! We are the Lord of people!"

When Abraham ﷺ said, "My Lord gives life and kills," Nimrod said, "I can do that, also." Empty head—he ordered two slaves to be brought, one to be killed and the other to be let free. Abraham ﷺ didn't argue but said, "My Lord brings out the sun from the East and sets it in the West. You

put it down in the East if you are the Lord!" And then Nimrod was surprised and astonished.[57]

Most people think that happiness for a person is to do everything as
he likes. (Ladies more than men want everything as they like, even changing their noses and everything. Devils are making so many pictures, and
they think that if they dress like them, they are going to *be* like them.) But it
is not happiness if everything is suited to your will. If you can put your will
in agreement with the Divine Will, *that* is happiness. *To agree with that One's
Will gives you happiness.*

That is the most important practice in every religion and in Islam: to
submit to the Will of the Lord, Almighty Allah, and the goal of the
Naqshbandi Order is to make people in agreement with the Divine Will.
Fasting, praying, washing for prayers is easy, but most important is to be
pleased and to agree with the Divine Will. That is, to be pleased with the
Lord, Almighty Allah, and that makes your Lord pleased with you.

Moses ﷺ was that one among all the prophets who was appointed to
speak with the Lord, Almighty Allah. He was greatly honored, but he
spoke to Him on Mount Sinai. But our Prophet ﷺ spoke with the Lord
Almighty on His Divine Throne. And we are all from his nation, believers
or unbelievers.[58]

And Moses ﷺ asked, "O my Lord, when are You pleased with me?"

Allah Almighty answered, "O Moses, make yourself pleased with *Me.*
Then *I* am pleased with you."

We must try to agree with Allah's Will. So many times our wills are
contrary to His Will; we want to stop His Will and let our will go on, so
many times. But the Prophet ﷺ says, "The one who is against Our Will, he

---

[57]2:258.

[58]Because Muhammad ﷺ is the last in the line of prophets beginning with Adam and there
will be no prophet after him, everyone who has lived after his time belongs to his nation
(*ummah)*

is not of Us, he is not of *haqq*, truth." We must try to be suited to the Lord Almighty's Will. ▲

13: CONCERNING PRIDE AND DIVINE LOVE

The weakest creature is man. But he looks around and is proud, and fights with himself and with others and with everything, and even with his Creator, although he is the weakest creature. And he has been created to live peacefully and happily here and Hereafter. But we are choosing the way of fighting; we aren't choosing the way that reaches to peace and satisfaction and happiness.

Therefore, there is some sickness with people, a wrong vision. They may look with sickness in their eyes and may see green and say "Red," see blue and say "White." They have been shown the way leading to peace and eternal life, eternal happiness, eternal pleasure, but they are saying that that way is the wrong way, no good; looking at *that* side with all its fighting, troubles, wars, diseases, miseries, evils and devils, and saying, "Oh, that is a very good way!"

For fifty years I have been looking from East to West, and it is the same view: people running after evils and supporting the kingdom of devils. Still they are not becoming less in supporting the Devil, day after day giving more support to him.

Fifty years ago Satan was a king. Now he is an emperor, no square foot where his kingdom is not present. And who ever comes proudly to a place of worship is bringing the Devil on his shoulders—in churches and synagogues, and mosques, also.

Once a *wali* was praying outside the door of a mosque, and when he was asked why he was outside, he said, "I am rebellious. How can I pray in the Lord's house?"

Some people come after everyone else and leave first. Such a person, when he was asked why, said, "I fear that my Lord may tell one of His sincere servants to inform people about my badness. Therefore, I fear that they may kick me out, and so I leave quickly." But *we* are coming, too proud of our worshipping to places of worship, not thinking that our worshipping is to give highest respects to our Lord.

As much as you are able to make yourself smaller, the lowest one among creatures, the smallest one of all mankind, you may give the highest respect to Allah Almighty. If you are coming proud, you are giving respect to yourself only.

We are following the ways of devils. First those people who were sent prophets and messengers, lost their way and Allah sent them away from their homeland. They were servants honored for holy lands. Then Allah cast them out; they were not suitable. And for thousands of years they were scattered all around the world because they were proud.

Christians also are proud, not following the teachings of their prophets. Jesus Christ 亝 was keeping himself from this life's ornaments and pleasures. [They are saying that he was killed upon the cross, but actually] Jesus Christ 亝 went up to the Heavens;[59] no one could touch him. People are thinking that he was the holy Word of Allah but yet it was easy to arrest him and to put the cross on his shoulders to carry. No! He was surrounded by divine lights. If anyone had touched him, he would have been thrown from East to West, into oceans!

All Naqshbandi shaykhs were witnesses, also, that night, seeing him going up [to Heaven]. He was carrying a needle and the angels asked about it. He said, "I used it, on earth, for sewing patches." Jesus Christ 亝 used needles, but *we* are never using such a thing, too proud!

And now we are living in the last quarter of the twentieth century. People are more proud day by day, everyone wanting to be more proud individually, and nations, also, are saying, "We are a superpower." The

---

[59]3:55, 4:157-158.

function of religion is finished, devils going on. People are sick with a sickness, making all people crazy ones. If no divine help comes from the Heavens to this earth before the end of this century, no divine cure, then all the world will be a mental hospital, from East to West.

No laws, people eating each other, destroying humanity. We have just reached the most terrible days of mankind; terrible days are approaching. But we hope that some heavenly events will appear. Each time that mankind fell into a well of darkness, divine help came.

No more prophets will come, but we have been informed that holy ones will come. Otherwise, no effect from those claiming to be religious ones; they are useless. We need holy men whose hearts are full of divine love, heavenly beings, whose love belongs to the Lord.

We only need divine love to be put into our hearts. Otherwise, we can't stop fighting, the endless desires of our egos, enmity, envy and jealousy till divine love enters our hearts. Then everything else is going to be cheap and of no value.

One of the most bright stars in the skies of divine love was Jalaluddin Rumi, a very shining star in that sky. He was one of divine love's stations; his heart was full. Up to today, Western people are running to his tomb, visiting. No one goes there and takes nothing. Everyone takes *something.*

Once he was going around Konya. He had come from Central Asia, from sun-rising countries,[60] and he was going around that city. The way of prophets and saints is to get in touch from time to time with people. They must go around and look after the Lord's servants, to help them, because they are divine love power centers. They can transfer love. You can't feel it, you are still sleeping. When you awaken, you will know.

---

[60]Here, Shaykh Nazim adds parenthetically: "Europeans are fortunate people because their hearts are dreaming of being in oriental, eastern, countries. A misfortune for oriental people dreaming of being in the darkness of sun-setting countries. Good fortune for your looking to the East!"

There was a goldsmith in the market, and he took Maulana's [Jalaluddin Rumi's] heart to the Divine Presence. When Maulana began to turn, he went up.[61] And also in the goldsmith's heart came the love of the Divine Presence, and he fell at the feet of Maulana, asking to be his *murid.* Then Maulana shouted, "O people, take everything! I have just taken my slave," making a bargain.

We aren't asking for animals' love; you can find that anywhere. We are asking for divine love. Mankind needs those holy people to come and give divine love. They are prepared to come and pass among people, to give them love divine; they are holy ones, hiding, but they are prepared to give from divine Love Oceans. If only one drop falls on mankind, they [mankind] can give away everything [else].

When Maulana whirled, he was flying. That period is approaching— one year, two, or at most three years. From its roots, everything is going to be changed.

Advice for you: *Keep your hearts away from this world's temporary pleasures. Don't keep envy in your heart.* Envious people never reach the Divine Presence; jealousy makes people lower than the level of animals. *Be careful: don't be envious of anyone.* Try to make yourself belong only to your Lord, Almighty Allah. If you do, He will grant from His favors the drop of divine love. ▲

---

[61]When he whirled in the love of Allah, he levitated.

14: about restraining our egos

May Allah bless you to be supporters of prophets and holy people.

People are in two parties, one coming with prophets and their inheritors, the other group going against prophets and against *awliya*. And according on their enemies, prophets and their inheritors reach high ranks in the Divine Presence.

The father of mankind, Adam, when his descendants increased, called them to believe in Almighty Allah, but the majority of them became a big group of unbelievers. And when they became unbelievers and Adam called them to believe in his Lord, they were not pleased with him.

Unbelievers are never happy to be within limits. If anyone orders them, "Don't do that, do this," they are not happy and feel enmity in their hearts towards those people who tell them to do or not to do something. Therefore, many of Adam's descendants disliked Adam (A) and felt enmity towards him. They were thinking to do something bad against him, and they gathered in a big meeting to decide how they might kill Adam.

When they met, one of them came forward to address them. Then Allah changed everyone's language. Everyone spoke a different language and no one understood the other; they were quarreling, cursing each other, but no one was understanding. From that time, all those languages came, Allah protecting Sayyidina Adam from those unbelievers.

Anyone who comes to advise good things and prevent bad things gets enemies, fighting against laws, police. "No courts! We must be free!" Like in jungles, the most powerful ones can be the rulers.

Now people are asking to have such freedom, because we have egos. The Creator is saying, "O people, your ego always orders you the worst things."[62]

"Beware of dogs!" they are writing. You can control dogs but you never write, "Beware of egos!" We are feeding them, and still they are coming against us. The Prophet ﷺ said, "A friend who, as long as you give favors to him, comes against you; as much as you respect him, he comes against you. If you put him down, he becomes respectful to you."

"Who can such a stupid one be?" the *sahabah* asked.

"Your ego."

As much as you respect it, it kicks you and harms you. Now you are fasting and your ego is unhappy, hungry, but when you give it what it asks for, it shows too much disrespect to you, disturbing you .

The characteristic of our ego is always the same, from beginning up to end, and all the prophets came to say to people, "Beware of your ego!" Fasting puts it down, under control, a little bit. This holy month is a very good opportunity for anyone who is asking to get control of his ego.

So many people are coming and crying, "O Shaykh Efendi, my husband or my wife is doing something with drugs. He or she wants to stop but isn't able. What can we do?"

No control on themselves! You may control London, but it is not easy to control your ego; you may be the conqueror of countries, but for egos it is difficult. The most powerful, terrible, tricky enemy is ego! Don't think it is easy to take control of it.

The People of the Book, all of them, were ordered to fast; Moses ﷺ and Jesus ﷺ also brought fasting. But they changed fasting, their egos cheating them. They said, "It is difficult to fast. We only won't eat animal

---

[62]12:53.

food, just eating grains and vegetable food," their egos cheating them and taking their fasting away.

You can't make your ego agree with divine rules. In the holiest month, Ramadan, whoever can keep fasting as Allah orders, it is from *this* moment up to *that* moment; we are even looking at only one minute.[63] That trains egos and gives Allah's support, His divine help, to be able to control our egos.

Uncontrolled people are always disturbed by controlled people. For that reason, they came against prophets and *awliya*. ▲

---

[63]That is, in Islamic fasting, the period of fasting is very strictly prescribed. Muslims watch the clock to determine the exact minute when eating and drinking must stop for the pre-dawn meal, *suhur*, and when eating and drinking can resume again at sunset.

15: about accepting muhammad as a prophet

For 950 years Noah was preaching, and people beat him with sticks till they thought he had died. But the Seal of the Prophets 🌹 bore more than anyone else; during the twenty-three years [of his prophethood], he bore more than anyone. His Companions, the *sahabah*, also bore [so much]. And Allah honored him and his Companions, and gave him higher ranks than anyone else, here and Hereafter.

Still his followers are bearing, because unbelievers are fighting them and saying, "You are not good people." The People of the Book are also enemies, although we believe in Moses 🌹 and the Torah, and we highly respect Jesus Christ 🌹, and we haven't any bad intentions against them. But still they are not proclaiming the Seal of the Prophets 🌹 as a prophet.

How do they know that Moses 🌹 was a prophet? How do they know that Jesus Christ 🌹 was more than a prophet, and they accept Abraham, David, John, Lot, Isaac, Jacob, Joseph, peace be upon them all? What is wrong in the prophethood of Muhammad 🌹? *Tell!* How do you know that the miracles of Moses 🌹 are true and Muhammad's false—*what proof?* Yet they are denying it.

Through their books, they know. Moses 🌹, in books, was informing that another prophet like himself should come. And they asked Jesus Christ 🌹, "Are you that one?" He said, "No. He will come after me." But the envy of people is preventing them, because Muhammad 🌹 is not from their lineage. And he is *Sayyidu-l-Awwalin wal-Akhirin*.[64]

---

[64]The Master of the Earlier and Later Times.

And Sayyidina Mahdi will come, and Jesus Christ 繼 will pray behind him to our Lord, Almighty Allah.[65] Soon, Jesus Christ 繼 will come, and before him, Sayyidina Mahdi 繼 will come to make everything clear. With him, 124,000 prophets will appear to make *haqq*, truth, clear—one or two or three years. May Allah make us to be with them! ▲

---

[65]The praying of Jesus 繼 behind the Mahdi 繼 during Jesus' second coming at the end-time of this world is mentioned in a number of ahadith reported in the compilations of Bukhari, Muslim and Abu Dawud.

16: changing ourselves, the condition for receiving divine help

Muslim jinn can only be in contact and under the command of *awliya*, authorized people. Others [non-Muslim jinn] are like the terrorist people of mankind, hiding themselves; now non-Muslims among jinn are also escaping, hiding from others. First, all the jinn will give *bayah*[66] to Sayyidina Mahdi; second, he should appear.

Those terrorist jinn, unbelievers, non-Muslims, are afraid to be in contact with anyone from mankind. Here in this country [England], no one is to be found who is in contact with jinn, but they are claiming that.

If a person is in the sea, not knowing how to swim, he may catch at a snake without knowing. People, if in difficulty, if physicians and psychiatrists and courts are not giving benefit, are going to those people[67] and hoping they can do something, read something. That line of 'business' is now in every kind of religion—*business*, but it is useless, because the one who falls into difficulties must first look to himself for the reason for his difficulties and problems.

There should be so many reasons in his life's conditions. Without going to ask such things from such strange people who are claiming that they have extraordinary powers or control on people, better for them to go and change their life's conditions, because all traditions are saying that conditions appear according to a person's actions and characteristics and attributes.

---

[66]Pledge of commitment.

[67]Mediums, astrologers, palm readers, diviners and others who claim to have to have special knowledge of the Unseen or dealings with spirits.

You can't stop that river, everyone coming to such people who are doing business with such things, and they are happy with people's continuing with their problems. But in reality, they [those who are in trouble] need something from those people who have been appointed by the Lord, Almighty Allah, *awliya*. They never ask for profit; they get their payment from their Lord, free workers for the sake of Allah. And first they say, "Go. First you must try to change your conditions. Otherwise we can't help you."

We are now seeing people increasing in troubles. Fifteen days ago, a famous doctor gave a lecture about that terrible sickness coming on people, and everyone is asking what is the way of cure for the virus of that terrible sickness.

Every wise one would be surprised that people are asking for a cure. They are not thinking of leaving that abnormal behavior, that dirty, abnormal connection; they don't think of leaving that, insisting on it and asking for a cure, then coming to the shaykh and asking help. And I am like a person standing on a bank and a person is saying, "Save me!" I am reaching to him with my hand but he is not reaching with his hand. So many people are coming to me!

A person asked Rasul-Allah for his intercession. He said, "You must help me to help you by making so many *sajdahs*, prostrations." *You* must help, also; your hands are full but still you are asking to be given. Leave what you are holding and I may give you something else!

As long as people do not intend to change their life conditions, even prophets can't help them. People now need spiritual support, but it needs a support from *your* side, also. A ladder can't stand alone; the two sides hold up each other. People now need thousands and thousands of physicians and psychiatrists, but such people [*awliya*] are very rare, as Allah is mentioning. They are rare people; you must look for them and intend to practice through changing yourself.

I am addressing all suffering people who have never followed any prophet. *The first condition is that they must proclaim the existence of the One Lord and Creator.* If they do not proclaim it, nothing can be done for them. I am not speaking at the first step about prophets, but before wasting time and money and themselves, they must accept the Lord as their Creator and Master. That is the most important condition for suffering people.

Therefore, we must try to give something to people to make them believe in One God, the Lord and Creator—that He is in existence and looks after His creatures, and that he [the suffering one] is a creature and humble servant to Allah Almighty. That makes troubles come down.

Second step: When a person came to the Prophet 鬱 to declare his *Shahadah,*[68] the first thing he or she had to do was to take a bath. Cleanliness is the second step after *Shahadah;* everyone must use it when they are in need. After sexual connection or dreams, men and women must use it;[69] they can use it as a foundation, like the foundation of a builing. Then it is so easy to help them; we can give support to them. If not, we can't do it. They *must* fall down into darkness and difficulty.

Jews have that cleanliness, also. If they have lost it, they are responsible for losing the *shari'ah* of Moses 鬱.[70] And Christians are not using that order. Every heavenly religion has ordered cleanliness; then divine support comes and they should be safe from misery. But a dirty person is cursed; as long as he walks about dirty, everything curses him. *Don't run away from water!*

Those who are claiming to follow prophets must take more care of their steps because there are two poles on earth, good and bad poles. You

---

[68]The Declaration of Faith, "I bear witness that there is no deity except Allah, and I bear witness that Muhammad is His messenger [*Ashhadu an la ilaha illa-Llah wa ashhadu anna Muhammadu-r-Rasul-Allah*]."

[69]Islam prescribes *ghusl* (showering with *wudu*) as purification after sexual relations, wet dreams, and the termination of menstruation and postpartum bleeding.

[70]That is, what was prescribed in the original *shari'ah* or divine Law revealed to Moses for the Israelites, which is, by extension, obligatory on all Jews and also on Christians, since Jesus 鬱 was a prophet to the Israelites following the Mosaic Law.

must take more care. Our steps must be towards the good pole. You must control your steps, beginning with minutes till you reach twenty-four hours' control. And if you are a believer, you must not be a liar, saying one thing with your tongue but your steps saying, "You are a liar!" The one who deceives us is not from our nation. *Believers are not liars.* ▲

17: putting our Lord's will first, then making ourselves follow his will

We are trying to make people understand the value of this life. If not understanding that, you can't understand the value of the eternal life.

You must understand that mankind is not created for this life, but the Creator is creating them as divine deputies for an eternal life. When He honored us by making us candidates for deputies, it was not limited in time; it was an endless and unlimited honor.

Mankind are the most fortunate ones among creatures. Every creature in this world is just created to give benefit to mankind here and Hereafter. All creatures are glorifying the Lord and are happy at being in existence; they are keeping the purpose of their creation perfectly. Every creature is keeping the reason of its creation, following it, and never deviating from the purpose that Allah created it for. Only mankind are heedless about their creation and about their creation's purpose.

Allah Almighty created everything for the service of mankind, and finally it is all going to vanish. On the Day of Resurrection, mankind is going to carry responsibility and is going to be rewarded or punished. All others He is going to order to vanish and they will disappear in divine Power Oceans.

According to the honor that we have been given, we are carrying something of divine responsibility. We are thinking that we have will power and we can do everything as we like, but if everyone tries to do everything as he likes, he will finally regret it because his actions according to his desires are going to be punished here or Hereafter. Man must know that he is created to be his Lord's deputy; he must follow his *Lord's* divine desires and

Will. Then he will be successful in his life and reach real deputies' stations in the Divine Presence.

Every time a person follows his desires against his Lord's Will, he should be punished. If you try to put your will first, it is against His Will. He never likes His Will to be second and His servant's will first. Who can think that it is good manners to put His servant's will first and his Lord's Will second?

Mankind's suffering is mounting day by day and people are looking for a cure for their miseries, but they are looking only with a simple sheep's vision. Mankind is accustomed to looking as sheep look at grass, never trying to look deeply at what is the reason, collectively and individually, for suffering.

It is so simple. All the prophets, from beginning to end, are trying to teach people, "O people, you are servants and He is the Lord. You must learn servanthood!" A simple waiter in Wimpy's or Kentuky Fried Chicken or a pizza shop knows; he says, "Welcome! What would you like?" He does not bring something you don't like and say, "You must eat or drink this."

How are we servants? *You* are a waiter, also. Like you, he knows that he is serving you, learning good manners to serve you. If you go to the Hilton Hotel or the Park Hotel, they even do *ruku*'; if possible, making *sajdah*,[71] also, so gentle and polite.

But we are saying for the Lord Almighty, "No! My will must go on!" Adam only once tried to put his will first and he was thrown out. But we are doing it every day one thousand times; then we are looking at books to find a way out economically or sociologically or psychologically. People are all going to be crazy from reading and not finding a way out. So simple: *put your Lord's Will first, then make yourself to follow His Will. Then He will make*

---

[71]That is, to please their customers, they may figuratively bow *(ruku')* and prostrate (make *sajdah*), as in the Islamic prayer.

everything as you wish. He is saying, "You can't reach My pleasure by fighting Me. I am irrisistible!"

There is a way you must know: *O people, you must come to houses through their doors.* Everyone comes through doors; if anyone comes another way, he is caught by the government. Allah says, "You must come to houses through their doors."[72] He means, "O people, you may reach goals through doors. Every goal has a way. You must know the way, the door." If you want to go to America but the pilot flies to Turkey, can you reach America? Allah is not greedy, but you must know the way to ask. What is the best way?

Moses ﷺ, before revelation came to him, was a shepherd for a prophet, Shu'ayb ﷺ. Once he was with his flock, coming to a valley full of wolves and wild animals. He became very sleepy; as much as he tried, he couldn't make sleep go away. The Arabs say, *"An-naum as-sultan."*[73] You can't defend yourself; sleep *must* win.

Moses ﷺ was helpless. He fell down and said, "O my Lord, Your Will is first. I don't want to sleep but *You* want it."

He slept, and after a while he was rested and quickly stood up, fearfully looking at what had happened to his flock. He saw a gigantic grey wolf, putting its stick under its shoulder and guarding the flock, other wolves never approaching, fearing so much. And Allah addressed Moses ﷺ: "If you are as *I* like, I am as *you* like."

"Put your will down and let *My* Will go on. Then everything should be as you like." You must say, "As You like," for everything. That is the key for mankind to take troubles away. As long as you want everything to be as *you* like, nothing is going to be as you like all your life.

---

[72] 2:189.

[73] "Sleep is the ruler."

Prophets didn't come to make people be proud of empty titles; they taught people servanthood. The second part of the *Shahadah* says "'*Abduhu was rasulihu*, His servant and messenger."[74] He has endless favors! ▲

---

[74]["I bear witness that Muhammad is] His servant and His Messenger."

18: concerning familiarity

When the Last Days approach, time will run, passing quickly. We were waiting for the three holy months[75] to come, and Rajab arrived and passed away and joined so many previous Rajabs. Sha'ban also arrived and passed away, and Ramadan has also arrived and is quickly passing. Tonight is the fifteenth.

Grandshaykh Shah Naqshiband, the most important pillar of our Order, our Distinguished Naqshbandi Way, always repeated his Association to make his attenders more familiar with each other and with Almighty Allah. Association is the best way to reach familiarity between creatures, and then with the Lord Almighty. Prophets, all of them, did that.

Without talking to each other, people are wild animals, never going to agree. Egos never agree to be on the same level with others—impossible! If they are forced, they may do it, but inside, never agreeing. Everyone's ego wants to be singular in its station, never wanting a partner. Therefore, ladies, if anyone wears the same dress, never agree; must put on a different one from others to be a special one.

Allah, the Creator, gives from His divine attributes to His deputies. He just created each one of mankind unique; no one is like other ones. Their forms and characteristics are all unique.

Each one of mankind represents one Holy Name of Allah; each one of mankind is trained, physically and spiritually, under one Holy Name of the Lord, Almighty Allah. As we are created different, everyone wants to be

---

[75]Rajab, Sha'ban and Ramadan.

singular in his state. But Allah is asking from mankind to be familiar. Even though they are unique, He wants them to be familiar with one other.

Mankind can't live by themselves; we are created to live all together. Familiarity is one of the most important characteristics that we must try to acquire. Ego is wild, never wanting to be on the same level with others, escaping from being familiar with others. But we have been asked to reach familiarity with the Lord, Almighty Allah, and the way passes through being familiar with people. If you can be familiar with everyone, you may be familiar with Almighty Allah.

Prophets, when they made Association with people, peoples' hearts came in contact with the prophets' hearts. It is not easy to bring hearts into contact with one heart; must be divine powers and sources so that attenders' hearts can reach those prophets' hearts and be familiar.

Prophethood is from the Heavens. Prophets can address the hearts of people, and it is impossible for open-hearted people not to be impressed by prophets' hearts. Their hearts *must* affect the hearts of those people whose hearts are open and *must* have an impact on their hearts.

Simple people crowded around prophets, first because their nature is near to Nature, open, and quickly they were affected by prophets' speech. The simple ones, women before men, were affected by prophets' Associations, their hearts easily opening. And when their hearts met, familiarity from the prophet went around that group.

The first step of faith in Islam is familiarity, planted into hearts, and an important condition is to like for others the same as you like for yourself. You can't be a real, sincere believer until you want for others the same as you like for yourself. And if no familiarity, you can't want the same things for others.

You must meet in the heart of a big one who has divine attraction in his heart because that comes from Allah Almighty. If not reaching to such a heart, you can't be familiar with anyone. A simple one whose heart does not belong to the Lord can't carry people. He must be a high-standard one whose heart belongs only to the Lord.

Therefore, Associations with prophets gathered open-hearted people—not like some people, who knew that there would come a great prophet but envy closed their hearts, and even Association with the Prophet ﷺ never affected them. They said, "Our hearts are locked.[76] As much as you may talk, it does not enter." Impossible for a person to come open-hearted to the Seal of the Prophets ﷺ and to be with him for even a second, and not to accept him and say *Shahadah*. Sayyidina 'Umar ؓ for so many years locked his heart from listening to the Prophet ﷺ, and the day that Allah blessed him and he embraced Islam, he came with an open heart.

Until our days, it was impossible for a holy one to speak and an open-hearted person not to accept. But if a person comes proud of his knowledge, proud of his mind, he comes not to accept anything but comes to make *you* accept something from himself. So many people are locking their hearts against *tariqats*; they can't take anything. We are giving Association and one who comes with an open heart must accept. If not, leave him. The Prophet's ﷺ speech never affected Abu Lahab or Abu Jahl[77] because both of them came with locked hearts.

No one can reach peace and satisfaction without reaching familiarity. If that familiarity, *uns*, does not come to someone, no peace; everyone disturbs that person, becoming like a thorn to him. And if you do not train under a holy man's association, you can't reach familiarity. Ordinary peoples' standard never carries people but a big heart carries people. It is Allah's attribute; *He* carries people.

Everyone who has the same attribute as Allah may carry [others]. Such a person takes from the Prophet's ﷺ heart familiarity and knowledge, and peoples' hearts meet in his heart. Then people from that group become familiar with one other.

Important is not knowledge, but to transfer from heart to heart. I may speak from under the ground or from above the Heavens; important is to

---

[76]2:88, 4:155, 41:5.

[77]The most bitter enemies of Islam and of the Holy Prophet ﷺ.

be transferring from heart to heart. Don't look at my words but at my transmission.

We are asking divine familiarity through His servants. And at the second step, familiarity runs to you from every creature and from you to them. Wild animals do not touch familiar people. They are obedient and show love to those people.

Once I was with Grandshaykh, traveling in the countryside. We passed by a farmhouse and a yellow dog came out with its tail curled like a scorpion. It reached Grandshaykh. He touched it, and that dog played on the ground and ran back. Grandshaykh said, "He recognized me, no stranger." Even lions amidst deserts may come to those people who are familiar with their Lord.

Once 'Abdullah ibn 'Umar, the son of Sayyidina 'Umar, may Allah bless them both, went to Hijaz for pilgrimage, going with a long caravan of camels. Then all of them stopped, and he asked, "What is the matter?"

They said, "A lion is lying in the way."

Everyone was afraid. But he said, "Make my camel kneel down." He got down and went to the lion. When he reached it, he took the lion by its ear and said, "Don't be here! This is not the place for you. This is the way for *hujjaj*, pilgrims, to the Lord's Holy House."

You must be obedient and respectful, not quarreling with anyone. ▲

19: the common sickness of mankind: love of dunya

The Holy Qur'an is endless Oceans, from pre-eternity up to eternity. We may ask divine help [in understanding it] from Sayyidina Muhammad ﷺ, because it was sent to him and he was the strongest one among creatures to be able to accept the holy words of Allah Almighty. No one else is able.

Allah, at the end of the holy month,[78] gave His divine Message to all nations. He had given some revelations to the nations of earlier prophets but the Seal of the Prophets was sent for *all* nations. He was sent from among the children of Ishmael, but his prophethood is for all nations and for every period, for every time.

The most important book from the Heavens on earth is the Holy Qur'an, endless Knowledge Oceans and endless Wisdom Oceans. Anyone who needs anything, individually or nationally or universally, may find in it what he needs.

A question that is interesting to everyone: There are 6,666 verses in the Holy Qur'an, from beginning to end. And if anyone is asking what is the main teaching to people among those 6,666 verses, what the Holy Qur'an gives to people, what the Prophet ﷺ wants to teach people, it is important to know something about the teachings of the Holy Qur'an.

If we are giving an answer, the Qur'an says to people, "O people, you are not created for *dunya*,[79] but you are created for *Maula*"[80]—not for *dunya*,

---

[78]Referring to the fact that, the first revelation of the Qur'an came to the Holy Prophet ﷺ toward the end of Ramadan.

[79]This world.

because the Holy Qur'an gives a cure for the sickness of people and the sickness must be well-known in order to cure it. If you don't know a sickness, no medicine.

The Lord Almighty knows well the sickness of His creatures. All people coming to this life, their sickness is the love of *dunya*. Tasteless pleasures surround a person as soon as he comes here and make him sick. Love of this life is a common sickness for common people; only a handful of people are not sick from it. Most people *must* be touched by that sickness.

Through traditions, we know that whenever a child is born, Satan is looking. And when a baby comes to this world from the womb of its mother in the form of *sajdah*[81] and Satan sees that, he is very angry and slaps it, and the new baby cries. No one is safe from Satan's slapping except prophets. That is the share of Satan in everyone, and that causes that sickness.

While growing up, everyone must have a share of that sickness and they need a cure, and all prophets came to cure people from that sickness. It causes all troubles, wars, fighting, quarreling—the love of this low, temporary life, the lowest standard of life; you can't find anything lower than this life that we are in now. And we have been asked to reach to the highest level of life; we have been asked, through *awliya* and prophets, to come to the highest level.

But that sickness is very difficult to cure. Some people may be in the beginning of that sickness, but if it comes, that sickness, over hearts, no more cure.

O people, you have been created for eternal life, not only for this lowest, temporary life. Imam al-Ghazali, one of the biggest, king-sized scholars, whose good ideas and wisdoms are well-known in Western countries, also, was saying, "O people, if you could choose between temporary and eternal life, and temporary life was in a world whose buildings were of gold and whose streets were silver, everything with precious stones and orna-

[80]God Almighty.
[81]That is, in the fetal position, which, when the baby is on its stomach, resembles *sajdah*.

ments (you can't imagine anything so beautiful in this temporary life), and the other one, the eternal life, was like what you see here now, with stone buildings, what would be your choice—to enter this temporary life with gold and pleasures, or endless pleasure in an endless life with stone buildings? Which would you choose?"

Some people's heads are like footballs, nothing in them. If anything were inside, what would be their choice—to enter those dream cities or to live forever?

Reality is better than a dream. Better eternal life with this world's conditions than golden cities. But now people are not thinking. Truly, no time for our people to think about anything. People are just occupied with temporary works and enjoyments, daytimes occupied by work and nighttimes with imitated pleasures, because each night, nightlife gets to be more tasteless.

That gives depression to people. If you do it from time to time, it is tasteful. But if you must sit at a table from morning up to night, forced to sit there, it may last half-an-hour for someone who has thirty-two teeth.[82] Then, up to evening, twelve hours, what would he do?

People are not thinking. Every night your 'factory' is quickly making ready power for enjoyment, but if it is every night, it is going to be *dis*pleasure. Yet they are making it obligatory; they *must* go every night. They feel that they are pushed, their feet only walking. They don't feel any pleasure, they can't have any taste.

The Prophet ﷺ brought absolute wisdoms to mankind. He spoke a short sentence, four words in Arabic. Only a prophet could bring such jewels to mankind; common wisdom, but its application is for all. If mankind can keep that, the whole world is going to be Paradise. "If you visit someone every day, he is going to be fed-up."

---

[82]Shaykh Nazim adds parenthetically, "*I* may take one or two hours. I am taking one bite and seeing people finishing one plateful!"

He said, "You must visit from time to time. Then it increases love because too frequently makes love to be less. *From time to time.*" You may make longer intervals; then love is going to increase. When the time is longer, better.

A dervish came to his shaykh from time to time. And his shaykh asked him, "O clever one, why don't you come frequently?"

He said, "O my master, I don't want to be told, 'Don't come frequently.' That is the reason that is preventing me from coming daily."

If you want to increase in love, you must make it from time to time; if the interval is longer, it makes you happier and gives more love. Allah arranges everything to be from time to time. Even for ladies, to be more happy, He makes a period, a kind of fasting;[83] it makes you to increase in love. Through the Holy Qur'an, everything has been arranged according to this measure—like praying times, making you to increase in desire for your Lord.

The Holy Qur'an teaches how to ask for eternal life at full speed. When you are wasting desire for the eternal life on this temporary life's pleasures, it comes down. The more you 'diet' from this life, the more you have desire for the eternal life.

That carries you to the Lord's pleasure. When you ask for endless pleasures, ask for eternal life. O people, be far away from the endless desires of this life; it is dangerous! If taking a handful from Niagara, it is enough. A thirsty one thinks he can drink all of it, but, no; it is physically impossible to reach every desire.

When you are asking for *endless* desires, Allah may create a spiritual body and power; then you may enjoy endlessly in Paradise through a line of power. *Here* are only batteries, not enough for all desires; they need chang-

---

[83]That is, because women do not pray, fast, read Qur'an or engage in marital relations during their menses, it is a kind of 'fast' from these obligations.

ing. Down below, when the battery is finished—finished! Youngsters must not be cheated, so that they can reach to endless desires.

Keep yourself within limits: establish permitted actions for your life and forbidden ones. Even if all people do *haram*, forbidden actions, it never does harm to Allah, but *haram* harms *people*. You can enjoy yourself with *halal*.[84] *Don't run after haram!* It makes you unhappy! ▲

---

[84]*Haram*—forbidden, prohibited; *halal*—permissible, lawful.

20: making all our actions for the pleasure of allah

Bismillahi-r-Rahmani-r-Rahim. We are trying to do everything in Allah's Holy Name. The Prophet ﷺ said everything by the order of Allah Almighty, and he said, "O mankind, you must do everything for the Lord, Almighty Allah. Every action you do should begin with His Holy Name. A believer must try to make his actions important."

He meant to say that useless actions are not good for a believer. Anyone who carries responsibility must be careful even about breathing. Then how can he do something useless, making him guilty? He must be careful not to be guilty because it is no good for a believer to come into the Divine Presence guilty.

Believers must think about their actions, to do them for the pleasure of Allah Almighty. When actions are important, there should be a benefit for himself and for others. And He orders believers, if it is important, to begin it for the sake of Allah or for the pleasure of Allah. Even you eat because He orders you to eat and drink, to support to your physical body for His service, for worshipping.

Our Grandshaykh, may Allah bless him, said, "By fighting his ego and by the way of *dhikr*, glorifying, a person may reach a level at which he is not in need of eating and drinking, at which his spiritual power carries him without eating and drinking." But it is not a liked standard for *awliya*. If anyone had done that, it would have been the Prophet ﷺ. He would go one or three days without eating, but he prevented anyone from trying that, saying, "I am eating in the Divine Presence, but you can't."

In seclusion, our Grandshaykh was not in need of eating and drinking. When he was in Medina, also, and I was in his service, I ate and drank what he gave to me, but he did not eat.

When he was at that level, refusing to eat or drink, Shaykh Sharafuddin sent for him. He said, "I know you don't have to eat and you have no pain, never feel thirsty or hungry, but I am ordering you to eat and drink. Up to the end of your life, you have enough power from your soul, but I am ordering you to eat and drink and give *shukr*, thanks, for these favors."

Even in eating and drinking, people must consider their Lord's pleasure. Now in this holy month, we are not eating and drinking, but at breakfast time, *iftar*, too much pleasure! You must try to do that action in the name of Allah.

Don't eat and drink only for the pleasure of your ego! Throw ego back; be with your Lord, not with ego. If you are with ego, always punishment, terrible things, come; if you keep company with your ego, Satan comes to make a trinity. And every problem comes from that company.

You must be happy with your Lord, and when you are with Him, you should be happy here and Hereafter. When you are asking to be with the Lord, you must say "*Bismillahi-r-Rahmani-r-Rahim*," and say, "I am asking for Your divine support." *You must try to make everything worship, to do it for His pleasure.* That is our way of considering everything for the sake of Allah and not for ego's pleasure.

This holy month is a big opportunity to reach that level. We are living in the first standard of this life, in which our ego is partner with us in everything; even worshipping we can't do now without considering our ego's pleasure. And the Prophet ﷺ warned his *ummah*, his nation, "Be very careful not to make your ego partner with Allah Almighty," because ego is always lazy in doing any worshipping. But it is also not easy to do a worship without making one's ego pleased.

In His Book, Allah is mentioning so many pleasures for believers. He knows our egos best. I may say something to you and you may easily obey, but for little ones, children, we must give sweets to make them do something. For every level of our ego, Allah promises to give. If a person is on the level of ego, you can't move him for the sake of Allah, but if you say, "There are pearls," that makes that person to move. He thinks of that beautiful life of Paradise and finds will power to pray, to fast and do charities.

Allah, who makes us for the sake of Paradise, gives us Paradise as a reward. But we must try to pass that level, to do everything only for the sake of Allah, not asking for anything—*to do it for Allah*. That is the high level of the souls of prophets, who have perfect control on their egos; they know for which thing it is valuable to ask. Who would agree to be given a picture instead of a castle, or a picture instead of a man or a lady, or a paper that looks like gold? Anyone?

But for the eternal life, and here, also, we are asking for something for our egos. But we are not going to be pure servants without asking for anything except the Lord, Almighty Allah. The one who finds Him reaches every goal here and Hereafter, but the one who loses Him loses everything.

The prophets and their inheritors are not enjoying themselves with this world, and not with the next, also. They are asking for something else. Therefore, Allah will order angels to take such people to Paradise. But after a short time they will jump back to the Judgment Plain.

Each time one returns, Allah will ask, "Why don't you accept your Paradise?"

He will say, "My paradise is with You. I was not working for Paradise." Then a light will come and he will disappear, joining endless Beauty Oceans.

From endless Beauty Oceans, only one drop falls into Paradise, and imagination can never reach that beauty of Paradise (and one drop from that comes to our Mother Eve; from that one drop, all ladies take their beauty). Where did he go, that one who was never satisfied with drops? *They* know; we don't know, never using our faith-power to understand. He has disappeared into endless Beauty Oceans—disappeared, swimming, drinking. *And we are running after drops!*

Allah is sending drops one after the other. Therefore, the beauty of Paradise-people is going to increase. Here in this *dunya*, it comes down. But don't be worried. In Paradise, day after day, those drops will come to everyone's Paradise, making them, each morning, more beautiful and handsome.

Believe in endless happiness; don't make anything trouble your heart. Leave that darkness out; put that freshness into your heart. But that freshness can never enter your heart without the accompaniment of faith. When faith enters, pleasure appears.

We are trying here. For the *barakah* of this holy month, we are asking Allah to make our faith stronger so that sadness never comes inside. Try to be stronger in your faith! Look for every opportunity to make your faith stronger, every occasion for worshipping, ordered and permitted.

Secondly, try to take every forbidden thing away. The punishment for forbidden things is that sadness enters your heart; sadness is with people's doing forbidden things. Take away forbidden things from your physical body; then light and pleasure will come on you. Smoking and drinking are never a pleasure for those who do them; that sadness never goes from them. The one who wants pleasure must keep away from forbidden things. As they say "An apple a day keeps the doctor away," take away forbidden things and it takes sadness away.

May Allah forgive us. We are asking happiness for everyone. I am sorry for people destroying themselves physically and spiritually. I can't prevent it, I am so weak, but He may make weak servants strong. Take power over your ego and that power will come! ▲

21: GUARDING YOUR EYES

Allah Almighty is teaching His prophets, His *awliya* and His believers. Each group of people are students in the Divine Presence, according to their spiritual levels and according to their beliefs and according to their respect for the Lord Almighty. And we have been ordered to keep most high respect for Allah Almighty.

Perhaps a person may worship like the worshipping of all nations. If we can suppose that that one worships as all nations worship, *that* is respect. But to keep away from the smallest forbidden action is better than all nations' worshipping. More respect, *that* is.[85]

According to your respect, He is going to teach you. To leave a forbidden thing, even the smallest, is more valuable and lovely; that is the measure of respect. You may not be able to do all mankind's worshipping but you can leave that smallest forbidden thing. That is going to be more heavy [in the balance] on the Day of Resurection than all mankind's worshipping.

A person may go to Hijaz[86] now during Rajab, Sha'ban, Ramadan and three more holy months, praying and worshipping, and he is pleased; worshipping is most excellent in the holiest places. Then he may take a plane back to London, and when not guarding his eyes and looking at a hostess..!

May Allah prevent that looking! He may be there for six months or for forty years, but when going away, quickly Satan is hooking him.

---

[85]Referring to a *hadith* stating that to leave even the smallest part of what Allah has prohibited is better in the sight of Allah than the worshipping of the two species, humans and jinn.

[86]The area of Mecca and Medina.

That is most important for deceiving people and destroying their faith. Quickly a poisoned arrow comes into your heart and makes your faith to be poisoned. Satan and his armies are always fighting and taking your faith as a target. Keep yourself from poisoned arrows! Make a shield and protect yourself from poisoned arrows coming from ladies.

Respect is to guard against forbidden things; *that* is fear of God. At nighttime you are observing red lights; even though the government is not there, you must observe those green and red lights. Then, if you are observing those, why are you not observing green and red lights for Allah?

Every forbidden thing wounds and destroys real faith. Therefore we are never tasting real faith; always faith is wounded. I am saying this because it is the most important hook of Satan for all Muslims and all people.

For believers who know that they will be asked one day, Satan runs after them, to fix their eyes on forbidden goals. You may say, "O Satan, I now give you permission to take my eyes everywhere." That is the reason that Allah is not letting light come on our hearts' eyes. Impossible for a person to look at unseen worlds except through his heart's eyes.

So many worlds! Your Lord has granted you a private universe for yourself only. No partner there, not like this world; billions of partners for this dirty world. He has granted us a private universe, wider than this universe; we can enter it with one step. But it can't be seen with these eyes; must be seen with hearts' eyes. And if you do not guard your physical eyes, He will never give heart's eyes' lights. *It is prevented as long as you are wasting light.*

Some people are asking to be shown Paradise, like blind people asking to see the sun. *If you can't see it, must there be no Paradise?* If no light in your heart, no vision, you *can't* see!

Prophets are looking at unseen worlds; they are looking and seeing the Heavens, Paradise and Hells. If anyone keeps full respect for the Lord, Almighty Allah, He grants him to look and see.

But we are not looking; we are occupied by the things around ourselves, not taking care to look at our hearts, at ourselves. As long as you don't care to look at yourself, never is divine light granted to you. If you don't know the value of *these* eyes' lights, how can you keep *those* eyes' lights? Every grandshaykh is teaching to his *murids*, "If you are asking for light in your heart"—and every believer is asking—"then you must guard these eyes. That is important!"

Once we were walking with Grandshaykh through Damascus' Old City. Grandshaykh stopped and looked at the front of a shop. Too many things were there. Then he looked at another shop. He said, "This looking makes a person guilty. If looking without reason, without wisdom, why are you looking? You must ask what is the wisdom for that thing to be there."

Allah never creates anything without wisdoms. From the smallest part of universes to gigantic ones, everything is in existence by wisdoms. Without wisdom, even a single atom can't be in existence. *If you look at anything, you must look for a purpose.* If you are in need of buying, you may look, but you must not look for anything till you are in need, and your purpose must be for the sake of Allah. If you look for the sake of your ego, it makes you blind. *You must not do anything without intention, and your intention must be for the sake of Allah.* That is the first level of belief.

The second category of people are always looking for wisdoms; when they look, they must look for divine wisdoms. Wisdoms make people to approach the Divine Presence. Knowledge may move you on earth; like the tires of a plane, you may run on it, but not for getting up in the skies. Knowledge disappears when wisdoms appear. A person not reaching wisdoms can't rise to the Heavens. And the second category of people are looking and taking divine wisdoms, and trying to approach to the Divine Presence, saying, "*Subhana-l-ladhi khaliqa-n-nur, khaliqa-n-nar.*"[87]

And there is another category, also. They are looking and seeing the Lord's existence and manifestation in every person, seeing in everyone the divine representation of the Holy Name that trains that person. They are seeing the Lord in everything, seeing that He is All-in-All. They can't see

---

[87] "Glory be to Him who created light, created Hellfire."

anything except His divine manifestation; they see as if they are standing with the Lord.

If no power from the Lord, there can't be anything in existence. And if anything is by itself, it is a partner to Allah. Only He is by Himself; everything else is sustained by the Lord. Therefore, nothing that is sustained by Allah can be God. Jesus Christ 〰 is not God because he is in existence *by his Lord.* Each one of mankind is in existence by his Lord; each part of your body stands by its Lord.

That is a mistake, making Jesus as God. He is the Word of Allah, He exists by His Word. When Adam was created, He blew into Him from His Divine Soul. If taking that away, nothing would be there—finished! Everything is in existence by His one word, "Be!"[88]

The third category of people see their Lord's manifestations. Therefore, Jalaluddin Rumi, may Allah bless his sacred soul, when he met a priest in the marketplace and the priest bowed to that grandshaykh, Maulana bowed lower than him.

Our brothers, too clever ones, are not even giving permission for kissing hands! How can they give permission to bow to a non-Muslim? His *murids* said, "O master, that one is a priest!"

Maulana said, "We are more humble. He, that priest, does not understand, but I am bowing to that One who is making him be in existence."

Therefore, there are different categories of people. Some are looking and it is *haram.* For some, looking is *sunnah,* and for some *fard,* obligatory. The second category are looking at wisdoms; their eyes are shielded, protected. The third ones, they are prophets and saints. They can take heavy burdens from you. ▲

---

[88]The divine Word of command, mentioned in the following Qur'anic verses: 2:117; 3:47, 59; 6:73; 16:40; 19:35; 36:82; and 40:68.

22: finding light through the prophets and their inheritors

May Allah Almighty, by His endless blessings, give us from His divine lights and make our hearts to be lighted. He created the universe and the Heavens and the earth and ourselves, and He created light and darkness.

We are giving endless thanks that He created the Heavens and the earth and darkness and light. And He makes people for darkness and people for light.

Man is carrying, at the same time, darkness and light. Our bodies, without divine lights, are going to be dark. If those divine lights go away, this body is going to be in darkness, and to be destroyed and vanish.

Allah Almighty created man suitable for carrying lights. He sent His divine lights from the Heavens to people through prophets. There may be one thousand candles, but if you do not put fire, they never give lights.

Lights for mankind are coming from the Heavens. The one who reaches to that light, his heart may be the light on his candle, but if locking his heart, his heart is in darkness.

The first man and first prophet, Adam ﷺ, came with divine lights from the Heavens to the earth. He gave lights to his sons and daughters, but some refused and remained in darkness. At every time, Allah sent prophets and messengers to bring divine lights to people.

Even in the days of the Last Prophet, Sayyidina Muhammad ﷺ, so many people were locking their hearts from taking lights from him. One group came and opened their hearts, and the Prophet ﷺ gave from those lights and they were shining. The Prophet ﷺ described his Companions as shining stars in the sky.

The second group were from the same nation, the same tribe, the same city, but they were stubborn, insisting on not opening their hearts. They said, "Our hearts are locked to you. We aren't letting our hearts listen to you." And they passed away in darkness.

Seventy of them, who were the most stubborn, powerful people standing against the Prophet ﷺ and who never approached to listen, remained in that darkness, and their lives ended in the Battle of Badr (next Friday is its anniversary). Two groups of people came to fight in that battle: darkness people came to take away lights and lighted people came to give lights.

Allah gave victory to the Prophet ﷺ, and he won and defeated darkness. A handful of lighted people, three hundred-and-thirteen, defeated more than one thousand armored soldiers with every kind of arms. Those seventy of the greatest enemies of light were defeated and killed and thrown into an old well without water. That was the end for those who were fighting against light and against being lighted. But *sahabah*, who opened their hearts to light, they are in light here and Hereafter.

We call them *"Sultan"*.[89] Wherever they are, you can see their lighted graves and tombs—all *sahabah's maqams*.[90] You can visit them; their graves shine. Even though people of bad understanding are trying to make their graves unknown, always, daytimes or nighttimes, lights are rising. They can't take away the lights that appear among their graves.

Darkness people think that lighted people die, that they become dead bodies. But they never die; they only make a veil. They are living; they have reached their lights, they have reached real life. Prophets are never going to be dust in their tombs. They will come on the Day of Resurrection as they were on the day they were buried.

---

[89]In Turkey, the Companions of the Holy Prophet ﷺ are referred to as *"sultan/sultana"*—that is, the 'royalty' of the Muslim *ummah*.

[90]A *maqam* is a tomb, grave or site dedicated to a prophet, *sahabi* or saint.

All inheritors who reached eternal life, who reached divine lights, are only veiling themselves and going on to eternal life. But those who refused lights, they are going to be dust, death grinding them in their graves. They are in need of a new body for the Day of Resurrection.

From the time of Sayyidina Muhammad ﷺ, people have been in two groups. One of them accepts the light of the Seal of the Prophets ﷺ, saying, *"La ilaha illa-Llah, Muhammadu rasul-Allah."*[91] *That* is the key for opening hearts to reach real lights. Don't think that any other way can open hearts to let light enter.

So many people in the West are claiming to reach something of spiritual power, light, but they hate or have an 'allergy' to the name of Islam. They are saying, "We are reaching heavenly stations without accepting Islam. Leave Islam aside and give us something else!"

How should lights come without the key? They are only imagining it. If they are too proud to say *Shahadah*, from where are they asking lights? Shaytan is cheating them with some 'batteries'—"Look, red lights, green lights!" They don't know the kind with *divine* lights.

People are cheating themselves, saying, "Oh, very good! We have reached lights." But how does a person ask to reach divine lights while he is denying the Lord of mankind, the Lord of the universes? If you don't proclaim His unity and existence and submit to being His servant, how can you expect to reach to His divine lights? If they don't say *Shahadah*, it means they are refusing to submit to the Lord and to be His servants; they are only accepting their egos as their Lord, asking to reach to power stations only for the sake of their egos, to be more powerful, bigger. No meaning for their worshipping; they are worshipping their egos. And they are in darkness.

You can sit with them and quickly that darkness is coming on you; you can understand. People are rejecting the Seal of the s who brought light to

---

[91]"There is no deity except Allah, Muhammad is the Messenger of Allah," the Islamic Declaration of Faith (*Shahadah*).

more than one billion people. A huge crowd of people are still locking their hearts! Allah ordered the Prophet ﷺ to give them a chance till the Day of Resurrection approaches, till their prophet, Jesus Christ ﷺ, comes down among people.[92] "Give them a chance to think about your prophethood and let them try you."

Any unbeliever, if trying and opening his heart, quickly takes lights. So many brothers opened their hearts and those lights quickly came. That is evidence for all Christians. We are saying, "Come!" No one comes sincerely, with an open heart, without taking lights. He *must* take.

Still two billion Christians are insisting on not proclaiming the prophethood of Sayyidina Muhammad ﷺ, resisting. But, one after another, that resistance has begun to fall. The Prophet ﷺ says, "The one who can be patient may reach victory."

Islam is waiting patiently. They should see that for two thousand years they were on the wrong way, and they should repent and be sorry that they wasted two thousand years without reason. When the time comes, they should understand that it was just wasted.

We need, as Muslims, also, to open our hearts to more light. We don't need knowledge now. Knowledge that has been classified in books, except that knowledge that belongs to you individually, is like old-fashioned weapons; it is not effective against the attacks of Satan and devils. Therefore, scholars can easily be defeated by Satan.

We are need more of knowledge through increasing the light in our hearts. Lights can show us what is true and what is false. We are living in the time of discord, *fitnah*, and the darkness of discord is *too* dark. If anyone puts his finger in front of him, he can't see his finger.

It is so difficult to find true ones among devils. The first sign that they are devils is that they don't say *Shahadah*. *Shahadah* gives lights to everyone; the one who does not make *Shahadah* never takes lights, here or Hereafter.

---

[92]Referring to Jesus' second coming, mentioned previously and in Talk 27.

Here and in the afterlife, dark tunnels may be passed through only by the lights of *Shahadah*.

We are in such dark days now, and we are in need of light, we need lighted people. We may be in their Association even once in a lifetime. If you can be, once in a lifetime, they are keeping you, they are never leaving anyone who comes to them to extinguish his lights.

Don't think that their lights are from themselves. They are from the Prophet 變, and his lights are from Allah Almighty's divine lights. Allah supports the Prophet 變 and says, "Don't be worried that those people may blow out My Light."[93] *Who can extinguish the sun and more than the sun?*

At every time, you may find lights in holy men's hearts. If you meet a holy one only once and your heart is not locked up, your heart must take that light. *Use it!* With those lights, you may save yourself from every danger that is approaching mankind in our time. If no lights, your life is going to be in suffering and difficulty. Everyone must reach someone with divine lights. If not reaching, he must ask his Lord to guide him to someone with divine lights.

Now Muslims are too proud, more than anyone else; they are imitating Western people now and becoming very proud. But as much as that group may grow, it will never reach the Heavens—those people who are even denying the Prophet's 變 intermediation.[94] They are saying, "The Prophet completed his prophetic word and went away, died. Now we are only with our Lord." And if they are denying even the Prophet's 變 intermediation, how can they accept there to be an ordinary holy man? If they are saying, "No intermediation for the Prophet," how can they ask a holy man to be

---

[93]9:32, 61:8.

[94]*Tawassul*, mentioned in a *hadith* reported by 'Uthman bin Affan 變, in which the Prophet 變 instructed a blind man to pray for the cure of his blindness with the words, "O Allah, I make request of You and I turn toward You by means of Your Prophet Muhammad 變, the prophet of mercy. By means of him I have turned toward my Lord to accomplish for me this need of mine. O Allah, make him an intercessor for me" (Tirmidhi in *Mishkat al-Masabih*).

their guide? They are saying say, "No; *shirk!*"—big-minded people, knowing only three words: *"shirk," "bid'ah," "kufr".*[95]

They are not understanding that lights came on earth through the prophets. When the prophets went away, they had to leave someone to give those lights to people. They are making rules, saying, "Don't accept *tariqats*, don't accept Sufis, don't accept holy men!" Whom else shall we accept, then? There is no one else in the picture but devils. Huge numbers of Muslims are under the hegemony of devils, and anti-Christs should come, thirty before the big one.[96]

Therefore, O brothers and sisters in Islam, such ignorance has become common among people in our days that if anyone has a little bit of light, he can understand and distinguish. For anyone who wants to reach absolute truth and to reach his Lord's Divine Presence, it is enough. ▲

---

[95]*Shirk*: to ascribe divinity or its attributes to anyone other than Allah; *bid'ah*: an innovation in religion; *kufr*: unbelief, denial of God.

[96]Referring to the Dajjal or False Messiah, who will come at the end-time of this world, as foretold in numerous *ahadith*.

23: concerning allah's greatest name, the night of power, and sayyidina khidr

By our Lord's endless blessings, we have reached the second part of Holy Ramadan, a mercy for believers and for everyone. Even unbelievers are reaching mercy during this holy month.

The Seal of the Prophets 鬱 and his nation have been honored by this holy month. There is a *hadith* giving good tidings for the one who feels pleasure within himself when this holy month comes. Allah takes him away from Hells by being pleased with this month.

He is the Creator, and He makes times and places honored. Only *He* can do it; if He does not, no one can make any place sacred. Even if all people say that it is but Allah does not say so, it is not sacred. For time, also; for holy months, Allah gives that honor.

We have twelve lunar months. The most holy month is this month; you can't change it. Allah gives every month a kind of holiness but most to Ramadan. And He gives holiness, also, to some people from among His servants. If all people say that that person is Saint Luke, Saint Pancras and so forth, if that knowledge is given by their Lord to them, it is all right. If it is given by people only, those are empty titles, useless.

We must respect everyone. As a sign of respect, we may say "Saint Mark," "Saint Michael." And we may think about everyone that he may be a saint; prophethood is clear but sainthood is something secret. Allah honors them, and He likes everyone to give honor to those to whom He gives honor.

Mankind has been honored more than angels. For understanding this, Allah makes two angels around each of us and they are "honored angels";[97] two angels for one person because man has been honored, and, according to this honor, he is carrying responsibility. Therefore, two angels are recording our actions like that video camera, also recording my words. This tape is recording words but they are recording *everything*; they have such video cameras always.

It is reported in *hadith* books that when a person comes on the Day of Judgment, he will be given seventy records. Each of them is going to go on up to the end of his vision, and when that person looks at them, he will see his whole life reported and recorded on that record. Enough; seventy records will be enough for everyone's life. They are recording. Their records are more important than that video, recording even each piece of food that reaches our mouths for eating.

Muhiyuddin ibn al-'Arabi, a giant-sized *wali*, said, "O mankind, you have been honored. Therefore, give honor to each other. For each piece of food that reaches your mouth for eating, three hundred angels are working and preparing it so that it is suitable. That is a big honor!"

Allah likes, when He honors someone, for him to be honored by others, also. All of us come under the verse, *"Wa laqad karramna bani Adam;*[98] verily, We respect mankind, the children of Adam." Everyone comes under that title—every nation, every race, every color, every kind of people; under that title come prophets, saints, believers, unbelievers, obedient and disobedient people, all of them.

Everyone's essence is all honored. As *essence* we have been honored, but there come on people bad characteristics. You can wear good characteristics or bad, like clothes. If you wear good clothes and you are not good, it never changes your essence; if you dress in old clothes, it never changes your essence.

---

[97] 82:11.
[98] 17:70.

Therefore, Allah is looking at the children of Adam and giving honor to the children of Adam, but, according to our attributes, we are changing [from that honor]. Yet His mercy is coming on people, even if they are unbelievers. And He is asking from His servants to give their respect to each other. That is the most important point: to respect mankind, and He is asking from everyone to give respect to each other.

Allah hides sainthood and hides His saints (prophets must announce themselves but sainthood is secret). Allah Almighty hides His Greatest Name and He hides Khidr ☙, the Green Man;[99] He also hides the Night of Power,[100] and He has some wisdoms for hiding these important things. If He did not hide His Greatest Name that has miraculous power, if a person asked something for the honor of the Greatest Name, he would have to be given it immediately; miracles may be done with that Name.

Everyone may give respect for every Holy Name, and that Greatest Name works with another Holy Name. Only a few people may be given to know that Name, and we must always ask to be taught that Name. And when someone is trustworthy, he may be given.

Once a shaykh said to his *murid*, "This is a box. You must take it to that famous shaykh in this city. And this is its key. Take it to that one but don't open it, and give it to him. He should open it and then he should give to you the secret Name of Almighty Allah."

When the *murid* was going on his way, he heard something running inside the box and he became curious to look. Then he opened it, and a little mouse jumped out and ran into a hole and quickly disappeared.

He closed the box and went to the second shaykh. That shaykh asked, "Where is the key? Where is the trust?"

---

[99]The story of Khidr ☙ and Moses ☙ is told in Qur'an, 18:65-82.
[100]*Lailat al-Qadr*, the night in which the first revelation of the Qur'an was conveyed to Prophet Muhammad ﷺ by the archangel Gabriel ☙.

He said, "I opened it and that mouse escaped."

"O my son, you are not trustworthy for bringing even a small mouse! Then how can you carry the Holy Name of the Lord Almighty, because Satan may cause you to use it for something harmful and destroy everything."

[As we were saying], Allah also hides the Green Man, Sayyidina Khidr, may Allah bless him. Up to today, he has prayed *Tarawih*[101] here three nights. He informed me, and up to the end of Ramadan he will complete seven *Tarawihs* with us. When he comes to a *jama'at*[102] for praying, he gives from his heavenly powers to all the people who are there. When he comes, you may feel more pleasure and refreshment and happiness here.

Sayyidina Khidr ﷺ always has miraculous powers, always. He can say "Be!" for a thing and it will be. That specialty has been given to him from the beginning up to the end. He is still alive, and he is going to be the last one to die among believers. He will see Jesus Christ's ﷺ coming and he will be here for fifty years after it.

For forty years there will be no unbelievers, only obedient servants; for forty years the earth, all of it, will be for Allah's sincere servants. When that period finishes, another period will arrive, and unbelievers will appear and increase quickly. Jesus Christ ﷺ will go to visit the Seal of the Prophets ﷺ [in his grave], and there he will die. He will be buried in the vicinity of the Prophet ﷺ: Sayyidina Muhammad ﷺ, Abu Bakr ﷺ, 'Umar ﷺ, Sayyidina 'Isa ﷺ [Jesus]; under the green dome of the Prophet ﷺ, four graves.[103] On the Day of Resurrection, all of them will rise up and go to Damascus.[104]

---

[101] The special nightly prayers of Ramadan.

[102] Congregation.

[103] It is mentioned in *hadiths* that when Jesus ﷺ dies at the end of time, he will be buried in the same grave as the Holy Prophet ﷺ, Sayyidina Abu Bakr and 'Umar ﷺ. "The green dome" refers to the green dome of the Prophet's Mosque in Medina that covers these graves.

[104] The site of the Plain of *Mahshar* (Gathering), where, according to traditions, the Last Judgment will take place.

When Jesus Christ ﷺ dies and is buried, Allah will send a wind from Paradise. Every believer breathing it will die, a most beautiful death, smelling Paradise and falling down—all believers. Sayyidina Khidr ﷺ will pray over all of them and bury them, and then he will go, also, his task finished.

He is also hidden. Perhaps someone may ask to meet that holy one. He is a divine treasure, he may give precious jewels to you. He may use any form of mankind; you can't imagine them. He does not have to be in one shape; every kind of 'dress' he may use. Allah is asking from His servants to respect everyone. He might be *that* one.

We must respect everyone so that we may reach eternal happiness. You can't be Muslim till you want to respect everyone as you respect yourself. That, only Islam brings.

Allah also hides the holiest night, the Night of Power. The time when that Night of Power comes is within a limited period.[105] If you can see that manifestation and you ask for anything, you may reach it immediately. We must respect every night! ▲

---

[105]That is, during the odd-numbered nights of the last ten nights of Ramadan.

24: about *Ihsan* and Divine 'Programming'

Allah Almighty created man, and the creation of mankind is different from any other creature's.

Angels—we believe in angels, we must believe in angels. From the beginning up to the end, Allah ordered prophets to tell mankind that there are unseen creatures, angels.

Now, faith is based on something that is not to be proved by ordinary science; if you could prove it, then no one could reject faith. But the meaning of belief is different. By seeing, hearing and touching, it is easy to say that a thing is in existence, but faith requires belief in what you can't see, can't hear and can't touch. And Allah Almighty orders us to believe in angels. They are not impossible to see, but as long as people are on the lowest-standard level, they can't see them.[106]

Allah created angels from His divine lights. Unless they take human form, they are unseen. On some occasions, some *sahabah* saw angels in the form of men, but to see them in human form is difficult, also.

The Prophet 🌸 took his *sahabah* from the lowest standard of mankind to a level at which they could see angels, even in the form of men. In battles, they saw angels coming to support the believers against the unbelievers; in each battle they met angels. Without divine support, the believers were so weak in weapons and numbers.

---

[106]Shaykh Nazim here adds parenthetically: "There are jinn, also, not like angels, but they are also not seen.

It is known from traditions that several *sahabah* saw the angel Gabriel ※. Once, it is reported by many *sahabah*, they were praying with the Prophet ※. Then they saw a person coming inside.

He wasn't one of the known *sahabah*; it could be seen that he was a foreigner, a new one. No one knew that person. He was dressed in white clothes; no one's clothes were like that one's, so white you can't imagine. And he had a black beard, so black and shining that you can't imagine it.

He was a stranger, coming from some far country. But although he had to come through the desert, there was nothing on him of dust. There must have been some dust on his beard or his clothes, but he was so clean, no spot on him.

The *sahabah* were so surprised. He marched up to the Prophet ※ and sat down on his knees in front of him, putting his hands on the Prophet's ※ knees and asking him questions about Islam. And the Prophet ※ answered, about the pillars of Islam, the pillars of *iman*, faith.

He asked, like a teacher asking his student, and the Prophet ※ gave answers: "To believe in One God. To make *sajdah*, to give more high respect."

You can't give the highest respect without *sajdah*; it is the height of humbleness from a servant to the Lord, Almighty Allah. If all the treasures of the world are given in charity without doing *sajdah*, it is nothing, not the same as *sajdah*, so important a sign of respect.

Therefore, after *iman* or *Shahadah*, second comes praying. Each day, during each week, each month, each year, you must put your forehead on the ground and give your most high respect to the Lord, Almighty Allah. A person, if understanding the meaning of *sajdah*, never leaves it. He likes to do it for every occasion.

The one who knows about *sajdah* tries to do it more and more. A person was asking the Prophet ※ for his intercession, and the Prophet ※ said, "You must support my intercession by more *sajdah*," the means of reaching intercession and the mercy of Allah Almighty. If a person improves to real faith from imitation and he tastes the spiritual taste of *sajdah*, it is impossible for him to leave *sajdah*. They never leave it but want to do more and more.

"The third pillar is fasting during Ramadan for one month. Then charity, *zakat*, rich people giving to needy people; that is also obligatory. And to make *hajj*, pilgrimage," the Prophet ﷺ was saying.

And that one, the stranger, said, "That is right. You are correct."

Then he asked about *iman*, faith, its details (*Shahadah* is a summary; he asked for more details). "To believe, firstly, in Allah's Oneness and existence; secondly, in angels; thirdly, in Books coming from Allah, from the Heavens; fourthly, to believe in all the prophets, not making a distinction between them; and fifth, to believe in Judgment Day."

You must also believe in the sixth pillar: that everything in existence, individually and collectively, is just programmed by Allah Almighty, not coincidence, not chance.[107] (I am not occupying my heart with such words. My heart is already occupied; you can't occupy it again).

Everything is programmed, nothing is by chance. *That* we must believe. We see people programming something on chips; man programs thousands of words in the smallest space. And DNA is programmed; scientists know that that is a program for everyone and each one becomes like his ancestors. Each creature's movement is programmed. Every smallest bacterium in existence, where it is going, what it is doing, *must* be programmed—even atoms' neighbors in six directions, where they should be.

Allah keeps everything in its center by His divine power. Everyone's destiny is just programmed, and man has not been given any more understanding than simply to believe in that program. Your mind can't carry more than that; as long as you are imprisoned in your mind, you can't carry more than that.

---

[107]This is the belief known as *qada wa-l-qadar*, meaning that nothing happens except what Allah decrees, and that what He decrees could not have been otherwise.

That one [the stranger] listened and said, "Yes, that is the true answer." And he asked also about *ihsan*.

You can't find a word like it in any language except Arabic; no other language can bring that divine term. Therefore Allah chose that language for His Last Testament. Turks and Urdu-speaking people also all say *"ihsan."*

"Ihsan means to worship the Lord, Almighty Allah, as if you are in His Presence and see Him. But even if you do not see Him, He sees you. To reach that level of belief, that is *ihsan*," the Prophet ﷺ said.

The stranger said, "Yes, you are right." And he asked some other questions as a teacher asks and always said, "Yes, right." Then, when finishing, he got up and went away, not turning back to him.

He went out the door and the Prophet ﷺ said, "Do you know, O my Companions, who that one was?"

They said, "No one except Allah and His Prophet knows."

He said, "That was Archangel Gabriel. Go and look for him." But he had disappeared. "He came to teach you about your faith."

In whatever rank Gabriel comes and you see him, you are also clothed in that rank. All *sahabah* were clothed in those divine lights. Some people may be in need of this lesson as a cure for their doubt. When you believe in such things, Allah gives you from His endless blessings and favors. ▲

25: LIMITING OUR EGO'S ENDLESS DESIRES

Do you imagine that, among all creatures, any have been honored and blessed more than mankind? No; you can't say that there is another creature blessed and honored more than the children of Adam.

Allah Almighty declares in holy books, the Old Testament, the New Testament, and the Last Testament, the Holy Qur'an, that for everything, O children of Adam, We have granted to you what you asked.

Everyone asks from someone who is able to give; no one asks someone who can't give. You are asking. Some things man can give you, and that is also from Allah's grant, because if Allah does not move that person's heart, he can't give to you. Therefore, if you are granted something, it is right to thank that one who gives it to you. The Prophet 鑞 says that if you do not say "Thank you" to people, you aren't thankful to Allah. If we say "Thank you," it goes to Allah.

So many things man can't give. You must ask that Someone who *can* give, who has endless Power and Mercy and Favor Oceans, and He may grant endlessly. When you ask something, He should give.

He knows best about you, He knows if something is good for you or not. That little boy may ask to play with a razor blade; you would be crazy to give it to him, either wounding himself or others. *Something is given to you if it is suitable or right for you.* You can't know if it is good for you. You may cry, but He does not give if not good.

Sometimes man struggles with his Lord and says, "You *must* give," and sometimes He gives as a lesson to others. You can say, "O my Lord, I don't know. If it is good for me, give. If not good, change my heart from desiring that thing."

The prophets taught mankind about every kind of life conditions. Man is not allowed to ask to die. Everything—every condition, suitable or not suitable, all kinds of troubles, miseries—man is strong enough to carry. When conditions change and difficulties come and suffering rains on a person, he must not become fed-up and ask Allah to bring him death, not to mention not to kill himself (if it is forbidden to ask to die, what about to kill oneself?). If you have been suffering too much, you may say, "O my Lord, if you know that to live is better for me, let me live. If you know that death is better for me than life, then take my soul with faith, by Your favor," the Prophet ﷺ was teaching.

For everything, you may ask what is best for you to be given, and He gives. He knows the best for you. That is excellent manners, that is from the signs of prophethood.

When you are asking, ask with *adab*, with good manners. "When My servant asks something, no need to shout. Even if no one listens, even if the angels never hear, *I* know. And I am giving, I am just giving everything that My servant asks. Even though he may ask for something which is not suitable for him during this life, I am keeping it for him, to give to him later. I must keep My promise. If I do not give during this temporary life, I shall grant it to him in his eternal life."

Allah just gave you everything that you asked from Him, but He is keeping back some things for the eternal life. You should be happiest that day when He is going to grant that to you. "That is what you asked from Me. I kept it for the eternal life, to give benefit to you forever."

He says, "O children of Adam, if you ask for something which is not given to you, you should not be upset or angry or sad or unhappy. You are thinking only of that thing that is withheld from you, although it is only one grant, and you will be happy only with that one grant. But, O people, I am granting to you from My favors. If all computers worked to make an account of what I grant to you, it would be impossible!"

Allah is the Most True One for speaking the truth. If only one cell moves from its place, it gives endless pain to your body. Billions of cells in your body are in the right place. What a favor! You can't imagine what

Allah Almighty has granted us from endless favors. We are thinking only of that one thing that is *not* given to us, but when your tooth pains, you should understand. Man is such an oppressor, *kafir*,[108] denying the endless favors that he has been given.

Among trillions of creatures, He made you from mankind. Do donkeys complain? No, very happily braying! If he made you a bear, would you complain? Bears never complain! If He made you a rat? They are happy; cats are happy, also. But you couldn't be happy if He changed you to a rat or a dog. Why are you not thinking about that?

Among millions of creatures, among all of them, the most honored is *you*. Not enough? Each day we are fighting that He is not giving us all the gold in Central Bank, all for me! But you can't carry that; you can't eat the two portions of the food that you can buy with it.

In the Damascus market, when winter came, there were too many clothes coming from Europe to our countries. I saw a person wearing five, six, ten coats, and I thought he must be a rich one, but he said no, and I understood that he was a seller. No one can put one foot in a Rolls Royce and another in a Jaguar; the Queen also can't be in two castles at the same time. Man is greedy, not thinking, wanting all the money of Central Bank for himself. Night life finishes by morning. What can you take from this world?

Mostly, man is an oppressor and is denying endless favors. And the Prophet ﷺ is teaching people how they can be happy and peaceful in this life, saying, "O man, if you wake up and find money for that day's provision in your pocket, you must say that I am the happiest person on earth."

If you are not feeling well, that is a not good, an unhappy day for you. You don't have anything that keeps your heart from being occupied by fear of poverty or unhappiness. Therefore, if you have something for one day for your family, you must be happy.

---

[108]One who denies Allah and His favors, or covers and conceals the truth.

People who are never satisfied, dissatisfied people, never reach a limit where they say, "Thanks to my Lord. It is enough for me," to be thankful that He is granting us endless favors, and also pouring on His servants more and more. They should pass away from this life tired, and the tired one should be more tired in his grave, his eyes looking back at *dunya*.

There is time and space for us in the eternal life. You may ask, and you should be given as much as you may ask, more and more, Hereafter. Be patient!

Imam al-Ghazali—he is famous in Europe, also, as an Islamic philosopher[109]—mostly brought evidence as proofs for Western people's minds. "O people, what if a doctor makes his patient fast for three days without drinking, saying, 'If you drink, it will endanger your life, but if you are patient, after three days you may drink all your life'—should he be patient, or should he destroy his life?"

O people, this life is only like three days. Why don't you make yourself obey, restraining your ego? *No limit for your desires?* Keep desires limited in order to be free in the eternal life.

What says the mind of a clever one? You are seeing in our day, in the twentieth century that is finishing, that day by day people's desires are increasing, but any time they try to reach their desires, troubles are also increasing. The nineteenth century's people were more happy than the twentieth century's people. What do we need in order to say that we are happy? At that time, with three pounds they were happy. Now three *million* is not enough!

They were happy with one room and a horse. *We* are living in castles and flying but we are not happy. Make your desires to be less and you will reach happiness; otherwise, you will be tired from endless desires and never

---

[109]Here Shaykh Nazim adds parenthetically: "But we don't want philosophers. Their ideas are always changing—daytime and nighttime, young and old, winter and summer, hungry and full, always changing their minds. They are such proud people, never tying themselves to any prophets. They think that they can find a solution by their minds, never asking from heavenly sources solutions for mankind's problems."

get to be happy. That is the sickness of our century. If mankind do not keep minds in their heads, all the world is going to be a mental hospital, all of them crazy!

We are asking Allah to send a blessed one. One is enough, but he will come with so many blessed ones. You must keep a 'diet' if you want to reach to that one's time. Control, put reins! ▲

26: entrusting ourselves to our lord

Allah Almighty created man, and He made mankind to be in need of eating, drinking and resting. And He created every creature by divine wisdoms. Nothing is created useless; must be some benefit to people from everything.

Once a person was looking at a cockroach. He said, "For what was that created?" After a while he had a sore and no one knew any cure for that illness, putting everything on it. No help!

After so many days passed, a dervish looked at the sore and said, "It is so simple. No cockroaches in your house?"

"Too many!"

"Take one, kill it and burn it. Put its ashes on it and finished!"

Then that man made *sajdah* and said, "O my Lord, I will never interfere in Your Will any more."

If even any kind of creature disappears, there must be a balance in nature. Everything is created to make a balance for the life of mankind. Other creatures are not important, important is mankind.

Allah Almighty created angels. They are not in need of eating, drinking; no sleep, no tiring. But we need; mankind is created in need of everything. Breathing, also; He could have created man without breathing, but He made, in twenty-four hours, 24,000 breaths.

Every breath is by the Lord's command, not in our hands, to show that you are under supreme control. When you sleep, who makes you to breathe, your inner organs to work? Who is that One? And with each breath you are saying *"Hu"*; you *must* say it. (Therefore Allah made the English language universal, always saying "Who").

Man represents the Lord Almighty, and He gives from His divine attributes to man. Pride is for the Lord only, not for slaves. Only He is proud, the Most Proud One. He has rights to be proud, but of what are *you* proud?

Pharaoh was proud of what? Every forty days he only went to the toilet once; therefore he thought he was something. Allah made us in need of eating and drinking, and in need of the toilet, also. No good for one to be proud who has to go to the toilet! For that reason, Pharoah claimed to be the greatest God.

Allah's attribute is that the one who claims something without its being among his attributes must be brought low. Proud people are not reaching even the lowest level during this life, and on Resurrection Day, all proud people should be under the feet of the one over whom they were proud, *must* be under the feet of that one. (O men, don't be oppressors of your ladies. Only ignorant people beat their wives and give them troubles. On Resurrection Day, they will be under their wives' feet!)

Then Allah Almighty sent a servant to destroy Pharaoh's kingdom and his claim to be God—one simple servant with one stick, not weapons. That stick had come from Paradise with Adam, and it went from one prophet to the other as a trust, up to Shu'ayb, Jethro 襚.[110]

When Moses ﷽ escaped from Egypt and came to Jethro, he made a contract with him to be his shepherd. Jethro could not see; [he was blind]. He said to Moses ﷽, "Go to that room and take a stick to use as a shepherd."

Moses ﷽ went and chose one. Jethro said, "Bring it to me." Moses brought it but Jethro said, "Take it back and bring another one."

---

[110]Moses' father-in-law.

Moses 🕮 went and brought another one. Jethro said, "This is the same one!" And Jethro was very angry. He did not yet know about Moses.[111]

And Moses 🕮 said, "Whenever I want to take another one, this one comes!"

Then an angel came and said, "No argument. I shall be the judge between you." That angel planted the stick into the earth and then said, "If anyone takes it, it belongs to him."

Jethro ran towards it but he was sweating and tiring; he couldn't take it. Moses 🕮 easily took it. With that stick, he could destroy super powers. (Those Russians need a shepherd and a stick, also!)

Then Allah said, "Go to that *edebsiz*[112] one and call him to be a servant to his Lord, Almighty Allah!"

Moses 🕮 did not say, "With which thing can I go?" Allah had said, "Go!" That stick was for *him* now. When throwing that stick, it became a serpent, opening its mouth.

When more than 200,000 magicians threw their sticks and made a terrible show on that plain, Moses 🕮, by Allah's command, threw that stick down. It became a huge serpent and swallowed all of those illusions, then opened its mouth as high as the castle of Pharoah and rushed on the castle. Pharoah ran away from fear, and from that day on, he had to go every day forty times.

That is the chacteristic of ego—to be proud. Allah makes us to be in need of eating, drinking and resting, and sleep is more powerful than the strongest man. Allah could have made eating once enough for our whole life, but He made us in need of eating several times a day to remember that we are in need of His provision.

---

[111]That he was a prophet.

[112]Mannerless, referring to Pharaoh, who was mannerless because he did not acknowledge and worship his Creator who had given him his powers.

In our time, Allah is making people also to be in need of drugs, pills, tablets—everyone; handfuls. "Why are you taking them?" I am asking. "If not taking them, I can't live."

Western countries' physicians are giving medicines you can't find in our countries. Patients are very upset, saying, "If this finishes, I will finish." Twentieth century people are basing their lives on tablets, yet they are disobedient. They can't live without these tablets, every color, every size; even for sleeping they need tablets.

Everyone in our days is using those tablets. They are too fearful that if they do not taking those tablets, a heart attack will come. From every direction, Allah is sending fear to people. Yet they aren't thinking of trusting in their Lord, not saying, when going to sleep, "O my Lord, I am entrusting my soul to You." They are trusting in those pills, not in peace to say, "My life is in Your hands."

That is the reason that people are falling into deeper depressions day by day, not connecting their lives to Allah, to their Creator; *that* is the reason. It is so easy! Who created you? *He* created you! You must give yourself to your Lord. "O my Lord, my life and death, my body and soul, are in Your hands." Then you can sleep peacefully and live happily.

That is the reason that Allah created man to be in need of so many things. Grandshaykh always said, "O people, do you know the most lovely attribute to Allah Almighty? It is to know and to say, 'O my Lord, I am in need of You for everything.' When you are saying this, He is so happy with you."

But we are forgetting it when we sleep and in the morning when we get up. "O my Lord, You created my soul and my ego. Only You can cure my ego's bad characteristics. I give myself to You." If you can practice [the advice in] this Association, you may find too much benefit. ▲

27: concerning mankind, the deputies of allah, and the second coming of jesus

When Allah Almighty, before bringing Adam ﷺ into existence, informed the angels, saying that I am going to create a deputy for Myself on earth, the angels had some knowledge that Allah had given them. They knew that there would be a deputy on earth, and *malaika*, the angels, were expecting themselves to be the deputies.

Then Allah declared, "I am going to create *another* creature. He will be My deputy."

The angels said, "O our Lord, are You creating a creature who will make *fasad*, dissension, and giving deputyhood to him, while we are worshipping You without doing anything against Your Will?"

Then Allah said, "You don't know! You are rejecting, you are not happy with that new creature. But *I* am happy and am giving My deputyhood to him."

It is written for mankind that they should make dissension, they should fight and do evil, they should follow devils and try to do everything against divine orders. But Allah knows best about His creatures.

We have been given, from the heavens, a soul. Our bodies are from this world, its material. The honor that we have been given has not been given to the angels. They only have spiritual being from divine Light Oceans.

If we hadn't been given a physical body, we would be like angels, also, always worshipping, nothing else to do. But our honor is our physical body. Souls come into bodies, and we have been ordered to take complete control of our physical bodies, to make them reach real deputies' stations in the Divine Presence.

Now we are candidates to be deputies, but Allah is asking from His servants to reach *real* deputies' stations. We have been given those real stations but they are still hidden from most people. Only a few exceptions have reached them and know their stations, but commonly, people have not reached them yet.

No one can know about that station completely till he reaches it. If a person has never tasted honey, as much as you try to give a description of the taste of honey, is it possible? A little child, as much as you try to describe the pleasure of marriage, can he understand? And those people who have reached real deputies stations—as long as you are far from those stations, you can never understand.

But Allah is asking His servants to know the way to make themselves reach those deputies' stations. Therefore He sent prophets to mankind, perfect ones who have complete control of their physical bodies and egos. The one who can take control of his ego quickly gets in touch with heavenly positions; if not, he is always at the lowest-standard level.

The angels were looking at the lowest-standard level of mankind.[113] At that level, they are fighting, killing each other, making their blood to run like rivers, doing every evil—the first, lowest-standard of mankind. But according to their beliefs and understandings, believers' life standards are changing, and according to their control over their egos, they are improving from first to second, third, fourth, fifth. But at the first level, they like to fight and disturb each other.

I was with my Grandshaykh at the holiest place in Hijaz, in Mecca, during the days of pilgrimage. We were making *tawaf*[114] around Holy K'abah. It was during the heaviest time because people were coming from Mina to complete their *hajj*, and it had to be completed in a limited time.

---

[113]Referring to the angels' dialogue with Allah when He informed them about Adam's creation.

[114]Circumambulation of the Holy K'abah, one of the rites of the *Hajj*.

shaykh nazim adil al-haqqani

And people were pushing and struggling with each other to make a way for themselves, like fighting.

Then Grandshaykh said to me, "Nazim Efendi, close your eyes."

Just for a second I closed them and then I found myself with Grand-shaykh at the top level among people. There, another group was making *tawaf*, but they were so smooth, polite and gentle ones, like butterflies. Then I looked down: they were still were fighting, shouting.

Above the second level is a third one, a fourth one. The K'abah is on earth but, in the same direction, above it, there are seven heavens, seven levels making *tawaf*. At every level of the heavens, there is a holy building of a different kind of level—not, like the Holy K'abah, made of black stone; those buildings in the seven heavens are made of the most precious jewels. You can't imagine that beautiful view; you can't look at it with these eyes. After that, there is the Divine Chair, *Kursi*, and then the Throne, *'Arsh*.[115] At each of them, at every moment, 70,000 angels are coming for *tawaf* and going. Up to *Qiyamah*,[116] there is no chance for the first group to make it again.

It was only to give an understanding to me that Grandshaykh took me up to the second level. All of them[117] are from mankind, but they have reached real deputies' stations. They have passed through that stormy space; their spiritual power keeps them making *tawaf* there.

Prophets just came to take people up to that level. All people were fighting the prophets; they were against their ways, their teachings, their attributes. According to the number of their enemies, prophets' ranks improved. Therefore, prophets therefore were disturbed and made to suffer by tyrants, devils; no one among prophets, up to his death, saved himself from the harm of devils or those who represented devils. But in spite of it, they tried to complete their messages; always they tried to proclaim *haqq*,

---

[115]*Kursi* and *'Arsh* refer to the limitless domains of Allah's infinite glory, power and majesty.
[116]The Day of Resurrection.
[117]Those making *tawaf* in heavenly realms.

truth, to make it rule everywhere, from East to West, and to make people servants to truth and to those people who represent truth.

[Yes], prophets were disturbed and harmed by those first-standard people among mankind. They like to follow their egos and do not like true ways; always they are happy to follow egos' desires and may even harm others. They don't think. Prophets came to prevent them from following their egos. Therefore they became their enemies.

We are asking to follow the ways of all the prophets. The Seal of the Prophets, peace be upon him and upon them all, just came on the same way as all the others. No difference among the prophets; they all came to fight and destroy devils, to make people reach divine stations. Therefore we are following the Seal of the Prophets, and it means to follow all the prophets, fighting devils.

Christians are blaming Muslims, saying, "Islam brought the sword. And Our Lord," they are saying, "was not a prophet."[118] They claim that he didn't come with a sword; they believe that people captured him and put him on the cross.

If a prophet does not show power, devils may kill him. Therefore Allah sent prophets with power, but not to use against good ones: against dragons and wolves, against wild animals. Their forms are the forms of men but their characteristics are animals' characteristics.

[After that], for forty years, no more devils, no more fighting. It should be in Damascus;[119] I am waiting for Damascus to open. You should come after me; you should meet Mahdi ﷺ and then we should be in the biggest mosque.[120]

---

[118]That is, they say he was the Son of God.

[119]As mentioned in *ahadith*, these events will take place in Damascus,

[120]Referring to the Umayyad Mosque in Damascus, formerly a cathedral, which contains the grave of John the Baptist, the Islamic prophet Yahya ﷺ. Here Shaykh Nazim add, " Each day I am [spiritually] with John the Baptist, one hour each day."

The Seal of the Prophets ﷺ gave information about it. He was in Medina, fifty days' journey by camel from Damascus, and he said that my nation will be there in Damascus, and there will be one of the greatest mosques of my nation, a mosque with three minarets, and my brother, Jesus Christ ﷺ, will come down on the east minaret of that mosque.

The Prophet ﷺ was in Medina when he said this. But, as he said, his nation conquered Damascus, and they took that big cathedral and made three minarets for it. As he said, up to today everything has happened—everything, just like the sun of the day.[121]

That day when Jesus Christ ﷺ comes with his sword, we should pray with him and then go with him to kill Dajjal. He should kill him. That day, for every believer, there should come heavenly power to defeat devils and evils. He should clean the whole earth of evil; his days should be like Paradise. Ask to be in those days with Jesus Christ ﷺ. ▲

---

[121]Here Shaykh Nazim adds, "Each day when I passed by there with Grandshaykh, he greeted John the Baptist, and he [John] answered his *salam* [greeting]. I heard it."

28: seeking help through patience and prayer

Allah Almighty is the Creator and He knows about mankind; He knows best. And as He arranged mankind to be both heavenly and earthly creatures, and to be His deputies, He arranged every condition that would be suitable for them to reach real deputies' positions.

From beginning up to end, in His messages, He mentioned what man is in need of to progress and to reach the real position of deputy. He also mentioned in the Last Testament, the Holy Qur'an, what we need in order to reach. In one word, *we are in need to be patient to reach those divine deputies' stations.*

Allah Almighty is asking from His servants to reach those positions. "O believers, you must ask help from Me. But, as the way of asking for My divine help, I am leading you to some practices, so that you may reach My divine help to yourselves."

For what are we asking help? We are asking so that by His divine help He may support us, to make us able to take total, complete control over our selves—I mean, over our egos.

If Allah says to you to go like this, ego must say the contrary. Allah created ego and said, "Come!" and it went back; He said "Go!" and it went forward, from the beginning going against Him. If you can't take complete control over your ego, it is not going to take you to your heavenly stations.

You must know what ego is. Allah created ego as a horse to carry us, to ride on it and go. Allah showed the example of our egos: when He invited Sayyidina Muhammad ﷺ to the Night Journey, first came Buraq.[122] The archangels Gabriel and Michael brought it under complete control, and the Prophet ﷺ went on it for the Night Journey.

When Allah Almighty gave the Prophet ﷺ, the honor of mankind, the honor of the heavens, the honor of the universes and worlds, from His endless favors, the Prophet ﷺ always asked Gabriel, "Is this for myself only or for my nation, for my *ummah*, also?" If Allah granted to him from His favors and gave him an honor, he always asked it to be for his *ummah*, also.

When he was born, his mother looked at him and his lips were moving. Now, for a new baby to speak is a miracle; it also happened when people accused Maryam ﷺ, the honored mother of Jesus Christ ﷺ, but Jesus spoke and refuted their accusations.[123] And the Seal of the Prophets ﷺ spoke when he was born. His mother listened, and he was saying, "*Ummati, ummati, wa ummataa.*"[124]

Christians say that Jesus Christ ﷺ was the most merciful one for mankind because he sacrificed himself for them. But we don't accept that he was a 'lamb' to be sacrificed for mankind. It is wrong; they have been deceived since two thousand years. It is not true.

The most merciful one was the Seal of the Prophets ﷺ, whether people accept it or not; reality is never changed by their denying. He was the most merciful prophet; perhaps he was the Mercy Ocean for all creatures. Jesus Christ ﷺ just took his mercy from the Mercy Oceans of the Seal of the Prophets ﷺ. And the Prophet ﷺ said, "Oh, my *ummah*!"

Who is his *ummah*? The Prophet ﷺ is the honor of all creation, the honor of mankind. He was informed that on the Day of Resurrection he would be given a flag, the Flag of Thanks. Whoever would be under that flag, he would be in safety from Allah Almighty's anger, in safety from the

---

[122]The heavenly steed upon which the Holy Prophet ﷺ rode during his Night Journey.

[123]3:46, 19:30-34.

[124]This means, "My nation, my nation," addressed to Allah, "and [O] my nation," addressed to his community.

seven Hells, the seven places where the divine anger appears. The Prophet ﷺ says, "From Adam and after Adam, all prophets will be under the holy flag that will be granted to me by the Lord of the universes. All of them—that flag will cover all the prophets and their nations. I am *that* one," says the Prophet ﷺ.

It means that he is asking for all mankind, with its unbelievers, also—asking from his Lord, Almighty Allah. But Allah is saying, "O My beloved Muhammad, the believers are for you. Don't be worried about the others. I am their Creator and *I* am carrying them!"

The main attribute of the Seal of the Prophets ﷺ is to be the most merciful one for all mankind, and ultimately all mankind is his nation. He fought against devils who made mankind suffer, he fought against those people who represented devils. Throughout his life, he always said, "*Ummati, ummati, wa ummataa.*" Everything he was granted by his Lord, Allah Almighty, he asked, also, for his nation.

When he passes over the Bridge which reaches Paradise[125] (he will be the first one who passes over that Bridge), he will say, "O my Lord, give safety and protection to my *ummah*!" He will be the first one who comes to the entrance of Paradise, the first to knock at the door of Paradise. The first guardian of Paradise, the angel Ridwan, will ask, "Who is that one?"

It will be said to him, "Muhammad!"

He will quickly open, saying, "O my lord, we have been ordered to open to no one before you. Welcome! Come in!"

And he will say, "I can't enter before my *ummah*."

Then Allah Almighty will say, "Let all his *ummah* inside. Open all the gates!" And all of them will enter.

---

[125] An extremely narrow bridge across Hell over which all mankind must pass on the Last Day.

If you want to be proud, be proud of being from his nation! Every-thing that our Prophet 🕌 was granted, he asked for his nation, also. And when Buraq was brought to him, he asked, "Is that only for me?"

And he was told, "O Muhammad, O beloved one, as you have, *they* have. For your honor, they have been given it, also. Tell them the condi-tions by which they may have that Buraq."

When you are able to take total control over your ego, then quickly that ego is changed to a Buraq, to be taken up. And the first conditon for taking control over your ego is that you need to be patient.

For the way to be patient, Allah was sending verses to His beloved servant: "If they want to be patient, they may use two kinds of worship-ping. O servants who believe in My beloved one and are asking to be with him here and Hereafter, use two kinds: use *sabr,* patience, and you must ask help for total control over your egos by the way of praying, *salat.*"[126]

That *sabr* is explained as the way of fasting. To fast teaches you pa-tience; without fasting, it is impossible to take control. If you are asking for divine support over your ego, you *must* fast; during fasting you may reach divine help.

Secondly, you must pray. Without praying, you can never get control over your ego, so that that ego goes away and Buraq comes. Don't forget these two important pillars.

Adam, the first man, ordered his children to fast and to pray, to make *sajdah.* Jesus Christ 🕊 was fasting and making *sajdah,* fasting and ordering his nation to fast. Christians have been ordered to fast as we are fasting, but they changed it and made it fifty days before Easter.[127] But if you are not able to control your ego, you can never reach divine deputy stations. And if not fasting, no control over ego! ▲

---

[126] 2:45, 153.

[127] While in Catholicism the Lenten fast is forty days, in the Greek Orthodox tradition it is fifty.

29: the importance of bringing beliefs to people

All prophets were tested and tried by their Lord, and every prophet was surrounded, and also their followers were surrounded, by devils and their representatives. Any time a prophet came and proclaimed his Message, quickly those devils rushed to surround him and defeat him and make him vanish so that their false kingdom could continue. Therefore, all the prophets and their followers were disturbed and suffered.

Allah Almighty knows best why prophets were surrounded by devils and what was the benefit of being disturbed by ignorant people. And anyone who is ignorant of prophets, he is a devil; anyone who gives harm and disturbs prophets belongs to devils and is their representative.[128]

That is the normal rule for believers. Whoever believes in Allah and His prophets must be patient in carrying devils. Prophets are the examples for mankind, and firstly they are examples for their followers, because their followers must try to be on the same path. Prophets came to give benefit to people—to take away harmful things and to bring them benefits. And benefit should begin for a person in his heart. Therefore, prophets began to work in the hearts of people.

The first benefit which must be given to the hearts of people is to make their hearts in peace. If no peace in your heart, what benefit can be given to you? Physically and spiritually there must be peace. If someone is spiritually disturbed, he can't be in peace physically. You must take rest through your heart; then you may be in peace physically. Therefore, proph-

---

[128]Devils or evil ones may be either of humankind or jinn, as mentioned in 6:112; 7:38, 179; 11:119; 32:13; 41:25, 29; 46:18; 72:6; 114:1-6.

ets came to give spiritual benefits. Physically they gave too many benefits also, but peace for people comes through hearts.

First, it comes to our heart if we believe. If no belief, no peace can be established in your heart. Belief is like water, the heart is like a pot. When you put water in it, so many fishes can live in it; if it is dry, nothing can live in it. And the elements of peace can live only through belief. Without belief, the conditions or elements of peace never live in a heart. Therefore, first all prophets tried to give real faith to the hearts of people. Then the elements of peace could live in them.

First, prophets tried to establish faith, to make people believe in Someone who is our Lord. Allah declares, "The one whose heart is full of *iman*, his heart is in satisfaction."[129] Nothing can give satisfaction to the hearts of people except belief in the Lord, Almighty Allah. Then faith is founded in your heart and your physical body is in satisfaction, and you can give others benefit. But mankind now is losing faith day by day, their hearts drying out and their physical bodies suffering. Nothing from around themselves can give them benefit.

When a prophet came, he established among the hearts of people strong belief in the Creator and then belief in the Eternal Life. These two pillars give benefit to hearts; then physically we are taking support and benefit from those beliefs.

When prophets asked people to follow them people attacked them and fought them because they were ignorant ones, standing against prophets, and prophets defeated them till they could understand or finally vanished. Each prophet was surrounded by devils and evil, and according to their enmity and the severity of attacks of those devils, divine support came to prophets. Also, as long as their followers were fighting devils, spiritual support came to them. Only, in the beginning, a little bit of patience is necessary; only in the first moments, if an attack comes on you, you must try to fix yourself. Then, when Allah sees that you are firm, He quickly sends divine support. Only in that moment, the first shock, you must keep your-

---

[129] 13:28.

self. That is important; then you can be victorious. Every time that distur-
bance came to prophets and their followers, when they were patient, they
were improving, step by step.

Prophets' ways are not easy, but they are honored ways. The most
honored group of people among mankind are prophets and their inheritors,
because prophets only want to give people benefit and to take away harm.
That is their aim.

Other people are asking so many things from this life. Prophets don't
take payment from people; they only give benefit here and for the Eternal
Life. But ignorant people are asking to reject them, defeat them, kill them.
There is a saying in Arabic, "If the one who is blaming you is ignorant, it is
a clear proof that you are on a perfect way." If an ignorant, imperfect one
blames you, good tidings that you are a perfect one.

The lowest-standard people (I don't mean peasants, servants, workers;
the lowest are those who have no control on their egos, who always follow
their egos) are always attacking them. They may be the richest or most
powerful ones, may even be kings, yet they are on the lowest level of people. The level of people in the Divine Presence is according to their characteristics, not according to temporary titles or golden clothes or crowns.

The lowest people disturbed the prophets—wild people, foolish, but
their attacks never made prophets to be fed-up with their messages. They
were continuing on their way. Noah, for 950 years, was calling people,
never getting fed-up. As long as they were disturbed by people, their ranks
were improving and their honor was increasing.

Everyone's intention must be to reach people with benefit, as someone who goes to a person to give an injection. That person may kick him
but the doctor is never angry with him. He says, "That is a sick person."
Prophets know that people are sick and they use their tolerance. Noah used
his tolerance for 950 years.

Once Yunus[130] was angry with people, and he left that country and escaped, and he said, "May Allah send His punishment on you!" Then Allah did not accept him and imprisoned him for forty days in the stomach of a whale. Allah never likes impatience. So many prophets were angry with their nations but they did not run away; therefore Allah imprisoned him in the whale's stomach. And he was crying, *"La ilaha illa anta!* I was such an oppressor to my nation!"[131] and then Allah let him out.

Our Grandshaykh, who is making me to speak to you from his knowledge treasury, is sending something to announce to you. Now, also, he is putting words in my mouth and teaching all of us:

Everyone must try to follow the ways of the prophets. What were their ways? To give benefit to people and to take away harm. That level of people has reached to being civilized. Under that level, no civilization; wild people, not reaching the horizon of being human.

Now people are generally asking for investment; they are living for that interest only. "How can I invest?"—that is their only idea and thought. If not of benefit for themselves, they don't say "Good morning," but if you give them a cup of tea, they may even bow!

From East to West now, all are such investment people. Five hundred years ago, an *'ashiq*[132] was writing poems, and in a famous one he complained about people. He went to a place and said, *"As-salamu 'alaikum,"* but people did not say *"Wa 'alaikum as-salam."*[133]

All people have the same sickness now. Materialistic-minded people have increased in Western countries and now are covering Eastern countries; the sickness of unbelievers now is coming on believers, also. Like kangaroos, we are running after them, but they are on horses, never satisfied. You may be given the whole world but you may look at the moon, to

---

[130]The prophet Jonah 𞸷.

[131]21:87.

[132]A lover of Allah.

[133]That is, they did not return his greeting.

take that. also. People have lost their good characteristics, have become like rocks.

All of you want to be good ones. The first condition is that you must try to make people good ones. To make them good ones, you must try to bring them benefit. To bring benefit, first you must try to bring them belief, even if they may defeat you. ▲

30: trying to be a good one and benefitting others

What goal should man try to reach? That is an important question: What should be the purpose of a man during his lifetime—*to be what?*

And that is an important question. For its answer, man must know his position in this universe; he must know about himself so that he may reflect and may fix the price for reaching that goal. Before everything, therefore, we must learn about ourselves, about mankind. Our first meditation must be on that important point.

If anyone asks who you are, you must know the answer. It is not an answer to say your name only. Do you recognize yourself? Not enough to say, "I am a British subject, living in London, working at the Zoo"; that is not an answer.

Who are you? You must answer to me about your position in the entire universe, the seen and unseen worlds, also. You must know who you are among creatures in this world and universe. And when you have learned who you are and for what purpose you are in existence, you can try to make a way to that goal and it should be easy. But if not knowing, it is difficult to reach to your goal.

As a simple answer to the question, "For what purpose are you striving, what do you want to be?" you must give a simple answer: "I am trying to be a good one."

This is as They are making me to speak. This must be the purpose in this life for everyone, to be a good one. And you can say that everyone claims that he is a good one.

If it is true that everyone is a good one, what about this world's situation? What about sufferings, difficulties, crises, wars, fighting—for what, if everyone is claiming to be a good one? What about devils and all evils? Must be something wrong. Either we are not good ones or this world is Paradise and we don't recognize it.

No one will agree that this world is Paradise; no. Then the second possibility is that we are not good ones. No, mostly people are *not* good ones, even running, like rivers, with evil. We know that now.

[Therefore], now we must try to change our badness into goodness, individually and collectively; we must try to change ourselves. And there is a verse in the Holy Qur'an, Allah declaring that a change is impossible till collectively people change themselves.[134]

If we know that we are in difficult conditions, it is something from Allah Almighty because He arranges our conditions according to our characteristics, whether we are good ones or bad ones. If we know that we are not in good conditions, there is a connection. It means that our characteristics are bad.

"If you are not happy with those conditions, change your characteristics from bad to good, and then I will change your conditions," Allah Almighty is saying to us. We are asking for a good life, to be good ones. If you are not happy to be good ones and are running to be bad ones, you should be surrounded by difficulties.

You, as a member of mankind's family, must try to be a good one; you must learn what are the ways that lead people to be good ones. Throughout our lives we are seeing those crossroads. One goes to good people's ways, the other to bad ones' ways. And you have been given enough mind to understand good ones and bad ones.

Throughout the history of mankind, good ones and bad ones have been working, have been in action, and at every time there is a handful of good ones but a big majority following bad ones. Particularly in our days,

---

[134]13:11.

every place is full of advertising for bad ones; everywhere you can find it. Everywhere they are working to make people follow devils and to support the kingdom of Satan; it is difficult in big cities to find good ones. Everyone, knowingly or unknowingly, is trying to support the kingdom of Satan.

We must look at our actions and, before that, at our intentions. Sometimes I am asking young ones, "What are you going to be?" Mostly accountants, because man likes money; some engineers, some pilots, some this and some that. Everyone's intention, in his profession, is to reach an enjoyable life, a high life-standard. Never have I heard anyone say, "I intend to be a good one for the community." *How is this community going to rise?*

What is this? Don't think that they are asking to be holy men; it never passes through their minds to be holy. To be able to be each night in the most important dancing place, where the most important people come, not to go to simple pubs (that is the lowest standard for them)—in their imagination they are asking for *that* standard. They are ready to use every means to reach such a high life-standard.

That is a sickness with all people. How can you think that these difficult conditions of our time are going to be changed? Perhaps there are going to be more complicated and complex difficulties. Everyone's imagination is to be the first and everyone else his slave or servant.

That is the twentieth century's sickness. Psychologists, psychiatrists, sociologists—all of them are not able to bring a cure for that illness. They can't until they can understand about themselves. Even religious people now have no ability because the same illness is with them, also; they are also asking for a high life. As the Prophet ﷺ informed us, there should be a time when religious activity is used as a means to material benefit.

Everyone is like a cell in the body of mankind: if a cell is ill, the whole body must suffer. Most members are ill. We are asking to give you something to think about.

Allah sent His messengers as examples; you must look at them. And you must look at the closest one to mankind, look at *his* life. He, Sayyidina Muhammad ﷺ, was the best one, the best example for humanity. As all the prophets tried to teach people how to be good ones, their lives just passing in teaching people to be good ones, the first example we can take from his life is that he lived his whole life to give benefit to others, putting people first and putting himself last.

He tried to reach people with benefit. When he went to his *sahabah*, they were first and he came last: "I always support you, I always look after you." If a person goes in front, he never knows what is behind him. He was looking and walking *behind* them.

And also on the Day of Resurrection, when all the prophets will fall on their knees—all mankind, even prophets—and they will ask only about themselves, only one person will fall into *sajdah*. The Honor of Mankind, the Honor of the Universes, of Creation, only he will fall into *sajdah* and will say, "O my *ummah*! I am asking for my *ummah*!" He will not enter Paradise until all his *ummah* go in. He will say, "Anyone else?" and the angels will say, "No." *Then* he will go in.

He said, "O people, you must do like me. Keep me as the best example for everything." You must try to reach everyone with benefit so that you should be a good one. The one who reaches people with goodness, *that* is a good one.

Each night, you may make judgment on yourself. Ask for evidence whether you reached at least one person with goodness that day. If you can say, "At least one," it is all right. If not, you must be ashamed and say, "I am not a good one."

New fashions from Europe are now coming to our countries, also. When you pass through a market, they are putting boxes for blind people, for animals, for handicapped people. *Do you put something there?* It is a sign of mercy in the heart to put even two pennies. You may say at nighttime, "Yes, today I put something there. If not even two pence, I am ashamed!"

We must try to be a good one in this life, not to have something written on a piece of marble in the graveyard, no. In this life, to be written in the Divine Presence as a good one is important. ▲

31: concerning seclusion and depending on allah for our provision

No one can be Allah except Allah. He is the only One. Those who are making *i'tikaf*,[135] seclusion, may be here *and* there for *dhikr*, also. I was with Grandshaykh in Medina for *khalwah*,[136] and he ordered me five times to be in Medina in Haram ash-Sharif,[137] going and coming.

It is important, if a person is asking to reach the horizon of mankind spiritually, to practice as all prophets did, according to *their* ways. We can follow their ways till we reach to our destination in the Divine Presence.

All prophets did seclusion. After that, they were able to reach to meet the archangel Gabriel. For a standard-level person, it is impossible to get in touch with heavenly beings; they must do seclusion to take spiritual powers, to be in control of their physical bodies. As long as our physical body is in control of our soul, it is difficult to get in touch with heavenly beings.

In the Holy Qur'an, Allah informs us that when Moses ﷺ was invited to receive the Torah, he was alone, in seclusion, for forty nights, and then Allah gave him the Torah. Our egos, if we are with people, won't be able to accept that divine manifestation. Therefore, prophet had to be alone, away from people.

Each year, our Prophet ﷺ, during the holy months of Rajab, Sha'ban and Ramadan, went to that cave. He was alone on Jabal an-Nur[138] when

---

[135]Spiritual retreat.

[136]Seclusion.

[137]The Noble Sanctuary, here referring to the Prophet's Mosque in Medina.

[138]The Mount of Light near Mecca. At its summit is Hira' Cave, in which the Prophet ﷺ was observing seclusion when he received the first revelation of the Qur'an.

Gabriel came, and if a person is alone, it is easy for heavenly beings to approach. Among all grandshaykhs, also, none reached his spiritual station without seclusion, and anyone who is asking for real life must keep that way. All prophets and saints kept that way.

'Abdul-Khaliq al-Ghujdawani, one of our king-sized grandshaykhs, was the *khalifah*[139] of Allah, and he was given that rank by Allah directly. He ordered one of his *murids* into seclusion to reach his real destination in the Divine Presence, and in his time that period was seven years; for fighting against their egos till being able to conquer them, they needed seven years.

When 'Abdul-Khaliq ordered, that *murid* prepared himself and went into that small cell. Then the Prophet ﷺ ordered his shaykh, 'Abdul-Khaliq, "Look after your *murid*. He is someone who may quickly reach his destination. Show him some important things. Don't leave him for seven years in seclusion."

'Abdul-Khaliq went and said to his *murid*, "Come with me." They went to a garden nearby and the shaykh stopped near a river. And a frog jumped out, a green one, and, with its tongue, three times took earth, soil, and went back into the water.

That grandshaykh said, "Did you see what he did? Did you understand what he did?"

"No."

"He comes out each day and takes his provision, three tonguefuls a day. He is afraid to take more, [thinking that] he may die because the soil may finish."

Then that *murid* laughed aloud. And the frog came out and laughed, also.

---

[139]Deputy.

With their miraculous powers, grandshaykhs can do anything they like; any miracle that the Prophet 🌸 showed is for grandshaykhs, also. A frog has no need to eat earth, but that grandshaykh was teaching, because that *murid*, from that evening up to the morning, had been thinking about his family and his children. When he was ordered into seven years' seclusion, if they sold all his property, it might be enough for only five or six years. What would their situation be during that last year? All night he had been thinking about that point.

That frog laughed, also. And that *murid* asked, "For what are you laughing?"

The frog asked him, "For what are *you* laughing?"

The *murid* said, "I laughed when I heard you were afraid that the soil would finish if you took only three mouthfuls."

Then that frog said, "I was laughing at your foolishness. That soil might finish if I took a long time, but Allah Almighty has promised you and your family provision. *How could it finish?* And you were thinking all night about your family's provision!" A shaykh can look at his *murids'* situations always.

O my pupils! Faith is based on a strong foundation: you must believe in Allah Almighty. It is not enough to say, "I believe." He may try you, whether your belief is real or not. And Satan is also attacking believers and asking to destroy their faith. And he has a method to destroy our faith.

What is tnat method? He comes to a person, as he came to that *murid*, to give him a doubt about his provision. When a doubt comes to a person, that doubt destroys belief in Almighty Allah.

He is the Provider, no one else. No doubt about that provision for you! But when doubt comes, no more belief for you, everything coming down.

Grandshaykh said how it must be, our belief in the Provider: If all the skies were covered with steel plates from East to West, and on the whole earth there was no more grass and only a single piece of rock, if any doubt comes to a person's heart about where his provision will come from, no more faith for him.

He has promised provision! Don't think that by working, planting, farming, *you* are bringing provisions. No! If Allah does not send provisions from the Heavens, no government will be able to give provision.

Here in England seven years ago there was a drought; no rain. I came by plane and saw all England yellow; I was surprised. The government was very upset; they thought about what would happen if everything was going to be dry for one more year and no one could live here any more. And I asked, "How are you alive? You have everything. Allah is the Provider!"

The government asked every religious group to pray for rain; it is an old, good manner of servants to pray for rain. And, *alhamdulillah*, the holy month approached and we prayed, also, and I think that for the sake of holy Ramadan Allah sent rain and that drought went away.

In Turkey now, big lands of many acres are dry. People came out to ask for rain. Allah gives; when they ask, He gives. But we must be humble servants to ask.

In Moses' 赤 time there was a drought, also. The Children of Isra'il came to Moses 赤 to pray for rain, and he went out with all the people. When we do that—old people and young ones, cattle and flocks, taking the little lambs away from their mothers to cry, and the people crying—then Allah sends. And Moses 赤 was wearing his coat inside-out.

They went to an area on which no sins had been committed, a clean area. And the people cried and asked Moses 赤 to pray.

No answer, no rain! Moses 赤 said, "O my Lord, I am asking from Your endless favors!"

Then Allah Almighty said, "O Moses, among your people there is a slanderer," someone who comes and talks against people to others. "There is one in that huge crowd. Because of that person, I am not accepting your *du'as*."

Then Moses ﷺ said, "O Lord, show us that one, to take him away!"

But Allah said, "O Moses, mind your manners! You are asking Me to show that person. Then *I* am going to be the slanderer! Don't even *show* that one!"

When that person heard that, he asked forgiveness, saying, "O my Lord, I never want to do that again." Then, when he had repented truly, clouds came and rain came, and the wheat grew taller than Da'ud's ﷺ height, and thick.

But there was nothing on the stalks, no grain on them. Moses was surprised and very angry. "O my Lord, what happened?"

Then Allah Almighty said (He liked to make jokes with Moses), "O Moses, you asked for rain, not for *provision*. Now make a place for a fire, an oven. Then make a fire in your oven."

And Moses ﷺ did. "Take a handful of grain and throw it into that fire to see My power!"

Moses ﷺ threw a handful of grain into that fire. Instantly he saw that grains were growing in that fire, and big grain stalks grew.

And Allah Almighty said, "O Moses, you must ask for provision from Me. I can make your provision grow even in fire!"

And Shaytan comes to destroy your faith by thinking about provision! *Without causes, He can give provision to His servants.* We are asking forgiveness for every wrong thought about Allah! ▲

32: the current degeneration of muslim society

May Allah bless us for the sake of this holy month! We are asking Allah also to grant us the good attributes that we are trying to reach during this holy month. Now it is easy. Then, after the holy month it is more difficult, but, with Allah's blessings, difficulty is going to be made easier.

First you must believe. Beliefs are the foundation of our faith. We must reach from imitated belief to real faith. Most important is to believe in Allah Almighty. Sometimes it is so easy, but for some complex people it is difficult. To believe in God is easier for simple people. Those who have reached the top level of educated people also may believe strongly.

Simple people's belief is no doubt strong. And top-level people have real evidence so that they can give satisfaction to themselves through their knowledge. But there is a middle level of people in mosques and churches. They do not really believe or live belief.

That level is dangerous for people. They need advice because they can easily follow good people and they can easily follow devils, also. At that level, people should be asked to follow good ones, to be connected with good ones. That is a dangerous level for common people.

During the Islamic era, from the beginning up to today, many *tariqat* orders lived within the community, teaching people and saving them from following devils and bad influences. Therefore, charitable people were building, in cities and towns and even in villages, *tekkes*,[140] hundreds of such

---

[140]*Zawiyahs, khanegahs* or *dergahs,* gathering places for shaykhs with their *murids.*

buildings for *tariqat* people, with a *masjid*, sleeping rooms, halls, schools and dining rooms, all of them free. And with each one was a shaykh, looking after and controlling it.

When people were free from work, everyone needed to meet his brothers, to listen to the Association.[141] Anyone can go to a mosque but mosques are only for praying, and people need to meet and be together. And after coming out of the mosque, Shaytan calls them. If no place to meet and to go to, Shaytan can easily catch them.

Now, all those good places, *dergahs*, worked excellently for centuries, but in our times people came against them, because as long as people could be there and learn something from some honored people, from holy ones, devils were always asking to take them away. And they reached their goal in the last eighty years. Now devils are controlling everything and are not leaving freedom for believers.

Everywhere now there is pressure in the Islamic world. The Christian world has more tolerance than the Muslim wold; we can't find such a possibility in our country. Everywhere they control you, always follow you everywhere, because we are *tariqat* people.

From that time, in the Islamic world, they have been against *tariqats*. When *tariqats* are forbidden and all *dergahs* and *zawiyahs* are locked up, where can people go? To coffee houses, at least. And coffee houses are centers of evil-teaching, primary schools for devils, giving the first diploma; you know the levels after that. But first are the coffee houses, doing every badness.

Learning centers for every evil, coffee houses! You can't find any good thing there; they are the headquarters of Satan. Therefore, from the beginning of this century, people have been under the complete control of devils. They are looking at newspapers and learning.[142] Everything you

---

[141]The shaykh's *sohbet (suhbah)* or discourse.

[142]Referring to the use of literacy in Turkey for reading newspapers, the majority of which contain sections of pornographic photos, as well as advertisements for all kinds of Satan-inspired activities.

may see, advertisements for evils; they are even using cats or dogs for advertising.

What are they asking to do; for what are they putting cats? At the least, they are occupying people with something without meaning—such stupid advertisements, people under their control. Everywhere—newspapers, one thousand per cent; one million per cent, broadcasting; one billion per cent in their books and films! And all of them destroying our belief in Allah Almighty, because common people have no defense against that, and top-level people also can't do anything against it; they are only a handful of people.

And common people are running after the ideas of communism and they are saying, "No God!" They are catching people through two ways, through their stomachs and through sexual freedom, making them unbelievers. Unlearned people may quickly deny belief.

When communism came to Russia, teachers came to the schools and asked, "Do you believe in God?" "Yes," said some of the pupils. Then they cried for sweets but Allah did not give them.[143] Then that *shaytani* teacher said, "Now ask *me!*" and they asked the teacher and he gave.

Common people are like children, like sheep. If coming to a river, sheep never enter it; the shepherd pushes one into the water and when one goes in, the others also follow. People have no minds; if they see one person doing something, they must do it, also.

That is a common illness. The Prophet ﷺ informed us that when the Last Days approach, my people will follow the People of the Book step by step. Even if my people see non-Muslims entering into the narrow hole of a fox, they will try to enter also.

---

[143]This and similar tactics have been frequently used by communists, missionaries and others. People are shown something which they desire, and when they express a wish for it, they are told to ask for it from Allah. When it is not given to them in response to their prayer, the 'trainer' then instructs them to ask him. He gives it and then says, "You see, God is not real, does not hear you, does not respond, will not give, etc. But I"—or, in the case of missionaries, Jesus—"will give it to you."

Once the Muslim world was stronger than Western countries. It contolled Western countries and Western people were trying to imitate it because the weak always imitate the powerful one. The East was powerful through faith. Because of that they felt powerful, not because of weapons; through faith they saw themselves as powerful. But now in this century, Muslim peoples' faith is becoming weaker and is going to be zero. They are saying, "We are behind, not yet advanced—backwards. We must try to do more like Western countries, to reach their technology." But Allah's wisdom makes them to be down. When they reach one level, the West has already reached another one.

Their faith is weak. They are asking to be servants to Western people, and Allah gave them the most precious part of the world—the most beautiful, rich and everything. But they are coming to the West to be street cleaners. I am always saying, "Go home!"

Allah honored us but we are not thankful. Instead, we are asking to be like Western people. No cure for that sickness till we leave those stupid ideas. They are like women, always asking for equality.

But they are never going to be equal. On the five continents, everywhere, Allah is putting people to be suitable for that place. Now you can't see anyone walking on his feet; everything is upset, upside-down. We need someone to put everything in order from A to Z; *everything* is upset now. Allah is saying, "O people, I gave you a mind to use it!" But they think it is most enjoyable not to carry anything in their heads, never to think. ▲

33: the time of sayyidina mahdi

When Sayyidina Mahdi ☺ comes, it is going to be a charity-less time because he will order all the treasures under the earth and under the seas to be brought out, and there will be twenty ministers from mankind over jinn. So many treasures will appear (good tidings for ladies!), so many—like hills, everywhere, Mahdi ☺ sending people everywhere to come and take.

If peoples' egos were going to be the same as in our days, we would run to them, but at that time we will be given very powerful spiritual desires and heavenly views are going to come into our vision. Therefore, no one will be interested in such kinds of jewels, material ones. There will be another kind of jewels.

The Prophet ☺ ordered giving good tidings about Mahdi ☺: "O scholars and learned people, give good tidings about Mahdi!" But I don't see anyone giving it. That is important because the *ummah* is in a narrow position spiritually. They need good tidings about the future; otherwise they think that there is too dark a future. But we say as the Prophet ☺ said about Sayyidina Mahdi ☺: The whole world must stop to meet him. *He is coming.*

It is good tidings for believers—not for unbelievers; they get angry. And each time they are get angry with Islam or *tariqats* or Mahdi ☺, Allah says to them, "May you die from your anger!" Unbelievers are making themselves unhappy. Happiness is for believers.

The Prophet ☺ says that Mahdi ☺ will ask whomever wants to take those jewels to come. One person will come from far away and ask to take from them before all the people rush at them, and he will go and ask, "From where can I take?"

Now, for the Government, for five pence they must sign five signatures. But the guardian of those treasures will say, "Get in!" taking no signatures, and that person will rush at them.

Shining gold! If any of our people saw that view, he would faint—twenty-two carats, not eight carats. Rushing, coming on his knees, putting them everywhere, all pockets full.

While he is on his knees he doesn't understand about carrying all that, but gold is heavy. When he wants to get up, he isn't able to, so heavy, and he slowly takes them out. And he looks.

Are people still sleeping, or have they died? Have they not heard that it is free today? Then he says, "What about me? If no one else is taking, for what am I so greedy?" Only you? Go and put it back! For what are you taking that metal, like a donkey?

I am giving the view from 'Headquarters,' as the Prophet ﷺ said. Prophets have the power of vision in their eyes like television. And according to the power of their belief, everyone may see the Heavens and Paradise and *Qiyamah* and Hells. When Sayyidina Mahdi ﷺ comes, everyone will see the seven heavens, the eight Paradises, the seven hells and *Qiyamah*. Man is created with such powers.

So many guardians for some papers or libraries! If there were such treasures in our time, you would have to bring nuclear weapons to guard them. But when that person wants to give back the treasures he took, that guardian says, "Go away! When We give something, we never take it back!"

At that time, no need for charity because *barakah* will be raining down. Allah will order the skies to give wholly *barakah* and will order the earth to give wholly *barakah*. Now people are going long distances with tractors. At that time, such places will yield hundredfold. If you plant one boxful, you will take seven hundred boxes, trees giving fruit twice each year.

Sayyidina 'Ali ﷺ said about the signs of the Last Days that there would come a day for people when they wouldn't be able to take anything from trees without medicine [chemicals]. Now people are using too chemicals to grow fruits. Therefore, through those chemicals such strange illnesses are coming on people that doctors are saying, "I have never seen such an illness." But when Mahdi ﷺ comes and says, "*Allahu akbar! Allahu akbar! Allahu akbar wa lil-Lahi-l-hamd!*"[144] all that will be changed.

No hypocrites will live at the time of Mahdi ﷺ; they must be taken away. The one who harms people spiritually or physically can't be in that time. The people living in that time will be like the cream on milk. When the Prophet ﷺ spoke about that time, the *sahabah* were asking to be with them, and Sayyidina 'Umar ﷺ said, "*Ya Rasul-Allah*, we would give everything to be one of them!" And the Prophet ﷺ said, "Your love for those people is covering them, and you should be with them, you should be witnesses."

We are hoping and asking to be with Mahdi ﷺ. Ask! If the Prophet ﷺ says, "The lifespan of my nation's people is mostly sixty or seventy years," I hope that if I live normally up to seventy, I must be with him, because it is too close now, his time. No one can imagine that light, that happiness, that pleasure for people!

No one will need that electric power, all technology taken away. Allah has made those unbelievers to be happy with that technology in order to know their Lord, but they are going on their knees in front of technology instead of the Lord. Therefore, that headache should be taken away and another kind of power should come down, a part of Paradise.

At that time, you may think but your movement is going to be speedier than your thought, and you should be at the K'abah or in the East or the West more quickly than your thought, Allah opening at that time something of deputy's honors—only *something*, because this earth can't carry even one person with real deputy's honors. You can't imagine those powers until you reach that time.

We were expecting to speak about something else today, but They are changing it, to say something about Mahdi ﷺ to be happy. If someone believes, he will see more and more, till his spiritual powers appear.

---

[144]"God is Most Great," repeated three times, "and all praise is for Him."

Charity now is more important; you may do now as much as you can. At least you may do, for supporting truth in our days—*more important now!*—*sajdah* and charities. What you are given for a simple charity, you can't imagine. It is the time for trading for our eternal life. Good tidings for the one who believes that when he gives, it will not become less. Don't be afraid! Allah says, "When you give for the sake of Allah, I give. I will not leave you empty, I will refill." ▲

34: using your heart to understand

We, mankind, must know more about ourselves. That is the most important thing for us: to know about ourselves. The Holy Qur'an is teaching us the complete knowledge about ourselves, and the Prophet ﷺ worked to give an understanding to people about themselves. And his inheritors, *awliya*, are working on that point, also.

It is impossible for a person to reach a level of real faith without knowing about himself, because without knowledge about himself no one can know about Allah Almighty. Every *murshid*, grandshaykh, has reached to understanding about himself.

We have been honored by the Lord of the universes, the Lord of creatures. But although we have been honored, most of mankind is arguing with their Lord. No other creatures are arguing except mankind; it is impossible, but *they* are fighting, making a discussion. And the Prophet ﷺ gave warning and said, "The one who shoots at us, if he puts an arrow and knows it, he is not from our nation."

Every activity, every action, that is against the Lord's orders or His Prophet's orders (whose orders are the same as Allah's)—whoever rejects or does something against divine orders, it means that that person is coming and shooting the Prophet ﷺ. "Whoever shoots us is not from our nation," he says. If you know something that Allah or the Prophet ﷺ orders and you are against it, it is dangerous. You must try not to be against it.

But we know it and we are fighting. At that time we are far from the Prophet ﷺ. That fight continues till you reach a high level of faith where you can control your actions. Therefore, we need to know about ourselves so that we will not be against divine orders.

But our ego always likes to fight against the Lord, Almighty Allah, like Nimrod. Our ego, if not accepting divine rules, means that it wants to fight. Your ego is such an ignorant one; it never gives real value to believing in the Lord, Almighty Allah. For ego, it is so simple a thing: it thinks it can easily be the *sultan*, the ruler, of the physical body. Always, if it finds a chance, ego is going to fight with the Lord, Almighty Allah. It is the most difficult one to agree, always against divine orders.

Most people cannot accept anyone else to be first; *they* must be the first. Each time prophets came, they fought against them. They looked first at what was his right to be a prophet: "What is your proof? What does it mean, revelation? Why only for you? Why not for us, also?" The most arguing ones are mankind. Even though they saw the miraculous things that prophets showed, still they did not accept and argued with them, never ending their arguments with prophets. They thought they could take them away and make truth disappear, and *their* falsehood would go on. For that reason they came against prophets.

Most argumentative, our egos! Mostly, people who have a [spiritual] sickness are more argumentative, and those who think that they are something, not accepting to be nothing, and those who don't want to be something but to be *everything*. V.I.P.—if he is a V.I.P., *I* must be a V.V.I.P.!

The whole *Shari'at*, divine rules, came not to give something to ego but to take everything from ego and to make it a slave, when it is going to declare, "I am nothing, I am a slave." If a person does not come down to a low level from his imagined high status, he will never reach divine stations and power; as long as you don't accept to be nothing, we are not giving anything. Allah is saying, "O people, I have bought all of you, I have paid a price. I shall give you Paradise and you are all for Me." Even if He did not buy us, we are for Him, also, but He is saying, "O My believers, I have bought you and I am paying with Paradise."

Until you stop arguing with your Lord, you will never reach anything. Therefore, *tariqat* teaches people how to stop egos from claiming anything. You must leave your will in the hands of your shaykh, first of all; then you may learn how you can leave your will in the hands of the Prophet 🌸, and then you may learn how to leave your will yourself in front of Allah. If not getting training at the first level, people are never going to be able to carry servanthood in front of Allah. If someone does not leave his ego in front of his shaykh, he will go in front of the Divine Presence with his ego and he will be thrown out.

Abu Yazid, the 'king' of saints, asked, "How can I come to you, O my Lord?"

He answered, "Leave your ego and come. Don't bring ego! I don't like partners."

Ego says, "You like something and *I* like something. You must be obedient to *Me*, also!" But if you leave ego as it likes, it never lets you do anything for the sake of Allah. It says, "No Lord for you except *Me*!"

You must be obedient always, *tariqats* are firstly teaching people. First-standard people must follow a guide; common people's natural characteristics are ordering them to follow a guide. Perhaps a scholar in Mecca may do *tawaf* by himself, but ordinary people need a guide for the first time until they reach the K'abah and know in practice [how to do *tawaf*]. So many scholars know about *hadith* and Qur'an, but their knowledge can't reach to real Islam, and Muslim scholars can't reach to the Holy Prophet's ﷺ presence. If not humble enough to take a guide, they can't reach their destinations in the Divine Presence.

When you take a guide, you must say, "O my ego, I am not listening to you now. Now I have a guide" (but ego is never going to agree with that declaration). When you take a guide, it is perfect to ask about everything. At the least, you must ask about three points: about marriage, traveling and divorce; at the least, *that* you must ask.

Not to ask [other questions] shows that the *murid* is improving, because when the shaykh gives Association, he gives for everyone's needs. Even though all mankind may be in that meeting, if he is an authorized one, he must be able to give everyone his needs. But for beginners, it doesn't matter if they ask from morning up to night.

We must be present with the shaykh, not present with body but absent with heart. If someone comes without heart, it is like barrels sitting. You must come with your heart; They know how to fill it. During that time, without questioning, everything reaches a solution.

When the Prophet ﷺ came, people came to ask. But they were foolish ones. If a prophet comes and says, "I am a man from the Heavens, from your Lord," don't ask with your ego! Put your heart in front of his heart and look; quickly your heart can understand. If anything is in his heart, it willrun to your heart; if not, if empty, nothing can you take from him, even though he may speak from *Jum'ah* to *Jum'ah*.[145]

For new ones, it is important: Use your heart. No one can cheat you. Grandshaykhs don't need advertising. Have you seen any jewelry shop doing advertising? But for soap and cheap things, too much advertisement, all London full-up! In the market I don't expect to find jewels.

If you have a heart, look and sit down. If that shaykh is correct, it means that he has a heavenly connection. If not, go away. Those foolish people, coming and looking at whether that is a prophet, never using their hearts! ▲

---

[145]Friday to Friday.

35: CONCERNING *Dhikr*

Ar-Rahman, ar-Rahim—no one can be like Him. His beloved servant, Sayyidina Muhammad 🌺, represents His endless Mercy Oceans, and each one of mankind takes his station in the Divine Presence according to the mercy in his heart. Whoever wants to know his station or his rank in the Divine Presence, he must look into himself at what is the amount of mercy in his heart for creatures.

The Prophet 🌺 is *Nabi ar-Rahmah*, the Prophet of Mercy 🌺. He didn't say anything from himself, but every word he spoke was also revelation.[146] We don't take anything from his life before the age of forty as being *hadith*, no; from forty years on he began to speak according to the Lord's will. Like Moses ﷺ, divine words were put into his mouth.

Therefore, when Gabriel ﷺ first appeared to him on the Mountain of Light, he told him to read, to recite. And Muhammad 🌺 said, "I am not a person who can read, I am illiterate."

Gabriel ﷺ embraced him. Then a second time he said, "Read!"

Muhammad 🌺 said, "I can't read."

And a third time Gabriel ﷺ said, "You must read, in the name of the Lord, who created."[147] And he began to speak according to the Creator.

Meanings were given to the Prophet's 🌺 heart and he spoke; that is the way that the Lord taught His beloved Sayyidina Muhammad 🌺. And each time that Allah granted to him something from His endless favors, he

---

[146]Meaning that nothing that he said came from his mind or ego but was divinely revealed or inspired.

[147]96:1.

always asked it for his nation, also, and Allah promised to give it also to his nation. But He put one condition: if anyone wants to learn something of divine knowledges and Allah teaches him, that person must give most high respect to his Lord, Almighty Allah. Then He grants to him from His wisdoms and knowledges.

What is that most high respect? Allah is looking at His servants. He is not looking at your outer appearance, no; not important whether you are a red one or yellow one or blue one. Allah makes your whole body for yourself. "Only your heart belongs to Me, so leave it only for Me. Don't let anyone else be there except Me. *That is for Me only!*"

We are fasting, and we intend to fast a perfect fast. How should most high respect to our Lord be? Fasting is a respect, and it is simple fasting by not eating or drinking or fulfilling other desires; we are leaving them for the sake of Allah. They are *halal*, permitted, at other times, but during the daytime in the holy month, you must fast from them. That is simple and first level respect.

You must fast by your organs, also. We must try to keep our organs from sins with our eyes, tongues, ears, hands orfeet (but we must keep our organs from prohibited things at every time, not only in Ramadan). That is higher respect to your Lord, Allah Almighty.

There is most high respect, also. Allah is looking at your heart, and the highest respect is to keep your heart only for the Lord, Almighty Allah. Who is pleased to see someone whom he never likes in his home? How should Allah be pleased with you if your heart is full of someone whom He never likes? *Try to keep your heart only for Him.* That is the highest respect.

It is impossible without *dhikr*. *Dhikr* guards your heart from anyone else. Shaytan and his representatives are trying to prevent people from *dhikr*. Those foolish people claiming to be Muslims are saying that it is is *bid'ah* (they know only three words: "*shirk*," "*bid'ah*," "*kufr*"[148])! Allah gives permission to do *dhikr* everywhere, in the mosque. *Allah gives permission;* in

---

[148]Ascribing divinity to other than Allah, innovation in religion, and unbelief.

the heart, also. The heart is the *bait-Ullah*[149] that Allah built; He honored you by making that organ His house. We are asking to go to Mecca to look at that House that Ibrahim built,[150] but you must look for His home in your heart first.

Allah says, "I am giving permission to do *dhikr* in My home," at every time to do *dhikr*, "*Allah, Allah, Allah.* . ." And the whole universe is answering; it is full of that *dhikr*. You heart also must say, with everything, "*Allah!*" But we are dead people, never-understanding people. *La hawla wa la quwwata illa bil-Lah il-'Aliyi-l-'Adhim!*

Guard that House within yourself by *dhikr* so that Satan can never approach. If a person forgets *dhikr*, Satan puts his trunk into your heart and uses it as a toilet, putting every dirty thing into it. People are complaining that such dirty things are coming to their hearts. Because you are heedless, Satan is making your heart a toilet. You are giving permission: "Now I am heedless, no one to make *dhikr*. You cancome and use it as a toilet." You *must* understand. Such dirty thoughts are coming that you may be ashamed to say them. Say "*Allah.* . ." and he runs away!

"How can I remember Allah the whole day long? Is it possible?" some foolish ones are asking. Do you think that when you fall in love with a beautiful one or a handsome one, you will forget the whole day, half of your heart there and half with me?

Allah says, "My beloved servants, they are always with you,[151] going and coming, talking and walking with you. Physically they are with you, but their hearts are always with Me." It is not easy; perhaps it is the most difficult thing to reach to that point. But try for some time, even in the daytime, to be with your Lord, Almighty Allah. Even if you are with someone else all day, when the time approaches, five minutes before *iftar*,[152] everyone must be ready: to be in *wudu* and sit towards *qiblah* and be with his Lord.

---

[149]The house of Allah.

[150]That is, the K'abah, built by the prophet Abraham ﷺ, assisted by his son Ishmael ﷺ.

[151]That is, among other people.

[152]Fast-breaking at sunset.

Allah Almighty honored the nation of Muhammad ﷺ with endless honors. When He addressed Moses ﷺ on Mount Sinai, He spoke to him behind seventy thousand veils. But He says, "I am so close to the fasting people of Muhammad's *ummah* at the time of *iftar* that only one veil remains." Therefore, that is *adab*, good manners with our Lord. Grandshaykh was sitting, before the time of breaking fast, for fifteen minutes or half-an-hour to be present with the Lord Almighty.

The Prophet ﷺ, during the Night Journey, when he left the archangel Gabriel and reached such a station as no one may be able to give a description of, out of the limit of minds—when Allah addressed him, he looked in front, looked in back, right, left, everywhere seeing his Lord. When you sit, you must try to make your whole self in the Presence of Almighty Allah to reach a feeling that your Lord is looking at you from six directions. If you do it for even a short time, you should reach to highest respect. Don't make noise and come and go! *Be with your Lord.*

[A line or more may be missing here.] That is the condition by which wisdoms feed your faith. You should be another person. Each night a dress of divine light may come into your heart, angels landing with light on your heart.

People are trying to learn something from books. During that short time, Allah may teach you. People are asking for knowledge for the sake of pride, to be something. And we are asking to be *nothing*. To move your ego out of existence, that is highest respect. Our 'Headquarters' has made me to speak on something most important for everyone. ▲

36: the importance of the night of power

Whoever is keeping Allah's orders should be happy on '*Eid*[153] because Allah rewards him. The one who was obedient should be in peace here and Hereafter.

In the last third part of Ramadan is the Night of Power, the most important night. Allah is hiding this night from common people, saying, "It is more valuable than one thousand months."[154]

Who can reach one thousands months' worshipping? It is eighty-three years. But Allah promises to reward whomever is respecting that holiest night so that we will not worship only on that night, because if it were fixed on one night, people would only pray on one night. The twenty-first, twenty-third, twenty-fifth, twenty-seventh, twenty-ninth—one of them may be the holy night.

The one who reaches that Night should ask for everything, for this life and for the Eternal Life. We must ask Allah to be pleased with us; throughout our whole life we must intend to make our Lord pleased. If someone reaches that, he has reached everything; if not gaining Allah's pleasure, all of life is going to be nothing. That Night is the most important and holiest night. You must make Allah pleased with you!

I'tikaf for the last ten days is *sunnah*, also. For every *jama'ah*, it is necessary that at least one person must do it.[155] ▲

---

[153]The Festival of Fast-Breaking at the end of Ramadan.

[154]97:3.

[155]That is, in each Muslim community (*jama'ah*), at least one person should observe *i'tikaf* (seclusion or retreat) during the last ten days of Ramadan.

37: trying to be good ones

We have been ordered to be good ones. And we are sitting here for what? We are sitting and asking from His endless favors to make our faith get stronger.

All prophets were sitting and making association, and those who were attending with them, their faith was growing and getting stronger. We are in need to renew our faith, *iman*; that is our purpose in meeting with people and asking from Allah Almighty's endless blessings. And which thing helps you to make your *iman* stronger?

When you are trying to good ones, that helps you. If your faith does not get strong, you can't be a good one; good ones always have strong faith. But ones with no faith, they are not strong; bad-intending and bad-acting people, no faith.

Bad actions and, even more, intentions, destroy faith. Actions are with organs; intentions are in the heart. And faith is also in the heart. Bad intention comes near to faith in your heart and destroys it; no more can that person taste the sweet taste of faith. Bad intentions spoil and poison faith. Impossible to correct our actions without correcting our hearts. And without correcting intentions, our hearts cannot be corrected.

As long as your intentions are bad, your actions are going to be bad and worse. *That* destroys your faith. The whole of religion revolves around that good intentions. If anyone has good intentions, he is on the right path. If a person has bad intentions, he may be inscribed as a Muslim or a believer, but he is not a real believer.

If you see wrong actions, look at the heart; must be something wrong in the heart that appears as bad action. If you look at your heart, you must find a bad intention that pushes you to a bad action. If a person intends to do some bad thing, you must know that faith has disappeared.

The Prophet ﷺ made everything clear. During twenty-three years, he was explaining the Holy Qur'an down to the very finest detail, as a doctor comes and students' eyes observe his operating with the finest scalpel. The Prophet ﷺ, during twenty-three years, spoke millions of *hadiths* about the meaning of the Holy Qur'an, because the Qur'an is for all mankind; as long as time and space go on, as long as life continues on earth, the Qur'an is for mankind. And its first explainer is Sayyidina Muhammad ﷺ.

He was saying, "A person can't drink and be a believer; a person can't do adultery and be a believer; a person can't steal and be a believer." Faith in his heart makes everything clear. If there is faith in a person's heart, it is impossible for him to drink intentionally. When he intends that bad thing, his faith goes on his head and stands over his head. His heart is in darkness; no more light of faith.

Then that person does a forbidden act. If death comes to that person while he is doing a forbidden act, he goes without faith. That is a fearful thing, because a person may worship one hundred years and at the end, if death comes to him and he has left the way of obedience, he has changed his way towards Paradise and gone to the way of Hell. Therefore, he must be taken to Hell.

Allah is not an oppressor. "Where did you find My servant? Whichever way he was going, take him *there*." Maybe for one hundred years he went towards Paradise and then he turned towards Hell, and Allah orders, "As he likes, take him to Hell!"

We must control our hearts frequently, and the Prophet ﷺ was asking, "O my Lord, *la taj'alna mina-l-ghafilin.*"[156] A terrible thinq may happen to that person who is heedless, as, at the end of thousands of years, Shaytan went to the way of disobedience and Allah's anger quickly turned on him.

---

[156]"Do not make us among the heedless."

Hell's way is under cursed arrows. Therefore, the Prophet ﷺ says, "Whoever shoots at us is not from my nation," and the Prophet ﷺ takes his guarantee [for that] from Someone. Cursed arrows fall on that one; each day his troubles and sufferings increase. Don't think that a curse comes like mercy.

Mostly curses are coming to people; *that* is making people suffer. But Allah promises to His beloved servant ﷺ, "Even if the whole world is under the divine anger and curse, those who are on the way of obedience, never should any troubles or misery touch them. They are moving on the way of obedience, the way of Paradise, and no curse can touch them."

We need to learn and to practice. We must look every time at our actions, whether our actions are suitable for being obedient or disobedient, and control them. Each day we have thousands of actions and breaths. We must control ourselves. As much as you are controlling yourself, Allah gives you more blessings, and more blessings feed your faith. And as much as faith is strong, you are able to be a more obedient servant, and obedient servants are good ones.

The Seal of the Prophets ﷺ made it clear that if a person wants to know about himself, whether he is a good one or a bad one, he can test himself. If you want to hear about yourself, you can go to an assembly of people, and then you can leave that group and go out. Leave your ear with them; your ear may hear what they will say about you. If they say about you, "A very good one," that is a test of yourself. You may find a witness whether you are a good one or not.

A good one must be merciful to creatures, to mankind, particularly. Faith feeds a person with mercy; according to your faith, your mercy grows and covers everyone. The most famous *sunnah* to follow is to be merciful to everyone because the Seal of the Prophets ﷺ was *"the Mercy for Mankind,"*[157] for creatures and for all the universes. He is absolute *rahmah*, mercy.

---

[157]21:107.

As long as you give mercy to people, your faith grows and you can be happy that you are a good one. With bad ones, no mercy; mercy is with good ones. Without having faith, you can't give mercy; according to your faith, mercy comes and fills your heart. When you have a line from Mercy Oceans, mercy never finishes; always that mercy runs to creatures through you.

You can think about poor people while you are restraining yourself and fasting—their being hungry, being thirsty; fasting also teaches us to be merciful to poor people. For fifteen days, they put an advertisement around London. You saw it, perhaps, written on it, "Give more power to the poor," and that is a Christian aid organization; they wrote that. They may advise people in that way, but for affecting people, there is no practice in Christianity.[158] The practice for understanding poor people is *to fast*.

It is obligatory for believers during this month to do some charity, to give *zakat al-fitr*,[159] to awaken mercy's sources in our hearts. Each person must give that *sadaqah*[160] before the 'Eid prayer. In Christianity, no [such practice].

People are like walls and rocks. If you don't force yourself to fast, to know what their condition is, you won't develop mercy for people. Ask to be stronger in your belief. As much as belief is strong, mercy for people grows.

Now *zakat al-fitr* is only two pounds, but if you like to give £25 or £100. . . ! Pakistani scholars are saying one pound. They are such greedy and mean [stingy] people; they must say two pounds at least and more, no limits. Give and don't be afraid! They have been given everything here, they are rich. Why are their scholars saying one pound?

---

[158]Meaning that although Christian groups urge the giving of charity during the Christmas season, at the same time they celebrate the occasion by feasting and drinking, never tasting the sufferings of the poor and hungry, as Muslims do by fasting for a month.

[159]The obligatory charity of 'Eid al-Fitr, the festival marking the end of Ramadan, equivalent to the amount of an average meal for each member of one's family.

[160]Charity.

Must be support for poor people! Christians may order charity for Christmas but they are only drinking beer and wine and whiskey. More than one billion people *must* give charity now.[161] ▲

---

[161]That is, for the 1.3 billion Muslims throughout the world, the charity of 'Eid al-Fitr is a religious obligation.

38: taking only as much as you need from *dunya*

The Seal of the Prophets ﷺ is teaching people, through every *hadith*, to reach that horizon where he is.

The Prophet ﷺ is not happy to have his nation to be on a lower level, asking for everyone from his nation to reach his most high level in the Divine Presence. Any *hadith* that he spoke—if anyone can practice that, that *hadith* takes that person from the lowest to the highest level. That is a wisdom that I learned from my Grandshaykh.

Everyone must respect the Seal of the Prophets ﷺ, and everyone gives respect according to his knowledge of that Prophet ﷺ. Each one's rank or value in the Divine Presence is according to his respect for the Seal of the Prophets ﷺ. No one can advance in rank without giving more respect to the Seal of the Prophets, Sayyidina Muhammad ﷺ. And you can't be a person who gives proper respect until your knowledge about that Prophet ﷺ advances and improves; everyone gives respect according to his knowledge about him.

Scholars know about the Seal of the Prophets ﷺ, but *awliya* know more than all scholars. All scholars' respect and knowledge all together can never reach one *wali's* knowledge and respect. And also for *awliya*, there are several different ranks and levels.

All the *imams* of *tariqats* respect that Prophet ﷺ, but the level of the Naqshbandi Order is the highest level of all orders. It is the most distinguished order among forty-one *tariqats*, all orders ending in the Naqshbandi Order. The knowledge of the Naqshbandi Order is the highest knowledge and its respect for the Prophet ﷺ is more than anyone else's. And how do they give value to the Prophet ﷺ and his *hadith*?

Grandshaykh was saying that each *hadith* includes something from Sayyidina Muhammad's ﷺ knowledge because it is part of the knowledge that Allah granted to him from His divine knowledge. He created His beloved Muhammad's ﷺ soul and his lights. He trained him five times, 500,000 years, and gave him *'ulum al-awwalin wal-akhirin*, knowledge of all beginnings and all endings; of everything created, the beginning and the end, here and Hereafter. He has knowledge about the creation of *mulk wal-malakut*[162]—of this world, heavenly worlds and everything coming into existence, he has been given knowledge. He is the main reason for every creature and for all creation, because Allah created all creatures for the honor of that one, that beloved one.

He is the only and single beloved one in the Divine Presence. "For his honor," Allah declares, "I created the Heavens, Adam, everything." If he had not been created, Jesus Christ ﷺ would not have come into existence; none of the prophets would have been created if he had not been created.

When Adam asked forgiveness from Allah, he asked forgiveness for the honor of Sayyidina Muhammad ﷺ. And Allah asked him, "How do you know him, when he has not yet been created?"

Adam said, "When my soul first came into my body, I opened my eyes and looked at the Divine Throne, and I saw written on it '*La ilaha illa-Llah, Muhammadu Rasul-Allah*,' and I knew that that one must be the most beloved one of Your creatures because his name is written next to Yours. He will be Your representative among all creatures. And I am asking forgiveness for *his* honor."

And Allah answered, "Very true. If I hadn't created him, I would not have created you or anything else. Just for his honor, you have been forgiven."

The most honor, *he* has been given, and all creation has come into existence to be an honor for him and everyone gets honor from him. His name is Muhammad ﷺ, the Praised One, throughout creation. Everyone

---

[162]The material and the spiritual realms.

must know and praise him; otherwise it is impossible to come into existence.

Everyone, according to his respect for him, is reaching a nearer rank in the Divine Presence. We are trying to give our utmost respect to him through our *salat was-salam*,[163] as Allah is ordering us to give our respects to His beloved Prophet ﷺ.[164]

He was teaching his nation, and through each *hadith* you can find ways to reach the highest level, which ends at beloved Muhammad's ﷺ level or station. Each *hadith* is an ocean of knowledge. All *awliya* are taking what they need of knowledge and wisdoms through his *hadiths*.

The description of this world came through *hadiths*. If you do not understand the Prophet's ﷺ description of this world, you can't save yourself from this world's dangerous *wadis*.[165] The Prophet ﷺ says, "O people, this world is for all people. All of you are partners in this world. Allah is apportioning for everyone according to His wisdoms, giving more to some, a little bit to some, and to some nothing." [Correcting himself:] Not *nothing*; they are taking their share, but minimum and maximum. So many different favors they have been given.

O people, even if you are given the whole world, if all of *dunya* is for you, you must take from it only what is enough for you. Don't take more for yourself! If you take more, it may be others' share. If anyone takes more than enough for himself, he takes from *dunya* a bit of its poison, a dangerous thing for him. No good; don't take! May destroy you physically or spiritually.

You can understand from this *hadith* the whole meaning of this *dunya* and its quality; it makes you be always at the edge of precaution. You don't know which thing harms you or destroys you physically or spiritually. If you take too much, it poisons you.

---

[163]Our invoking peace and blessings upon the Holy Prophet ﷺ.
[164]33:56.
[165]Valleys, low-lying places.

You can't take except what you need. There is no meaning of saving up *dunya* when you can't use it. But Shaytan wants everyone to make big amounts to save, not to put to use for mankind, not to give benefit. That is the worst characteristic of egos.

Meanness [stinginess] is like a tree and its branches are coming on earth. If a man is mean, he catches a branch of that tree. That tree grows in Hell; if anyone catches hold of that tree, it takes him to Hell. And generosity is also like a tree, its branches on earth. If anyone catches one branch, that tree takes him to Paradise. Even if not believing yet, Allah may finally take generous people to Paradise.

You must know about this *dunya* and take only your needs from it. If you take more, it is dangerous for you. Everyone can see so many rich ones, but they are never reach more than their needs. They are only collecting and holding; without payment, they are the guardians of collections. Then there comes a sickness into their hearts, never becoming happy or in pleasure. It is impossible to be rich and to be in peace; their hearts are occupied.

Shaytan comes and makes them afraid for their gold, their possessions that they want to keep only for themselves, while it is impossible. Shaytan comes and says, "Oh, tomorrow you are going to die. Your relatives will be too happy that you have kept all of it for them." And when Shaytan comes and says, "Look, tomorrow you may die," that is enough punishment for them.

For everyone who gives, Allah gives him pleasure and peace and enjoyment in his heart. Therefore, this month, for generous people, is the season of charity. The *sahabah*, the Companions of Sayyidina Muhammad 鷙, said that he was more generous than the spring winds that make everything wake up. The Prophet 鷙 says, "In the autumn wind, protect your chest." For the spring wind, you can open it to come in, as on trees, also; the spring wind gives life to everything and reaches everything. And the Prophet 鷙 was more generous than that spring wind.

The followers of his *Sunnah* may follow as much as they are able. That gives honor and pleasure and saves you here and Hereafter, and makes you to reach the highest level with the Prophet ﷺ.

Our egos are against everything that the Prophet ﷺ brings, but our egos are sick, ill. Try to cure your ego through the sayings of the Prophet ﷺ and to think about his *hadith*; so many wisdoms, taking humanity from narrow paths to high happiness, here and Hereafter. We are asking forgiveness for every action against *hadith*. ▲

39: the prophet's intercession on the day of judgment

Ya Jami'u-n-Nas,[166] Allah Almighty! Only He gathers people. Any time He wants to gather them, He may do it. Before this creation came into existence, He first created the souls of people; He gathered and brought them.

Each one of mankind was present at that meeting, and Allah Almighty addressed our souls. That was the Day of Promises. Everyone was present; perhaps there was no time and no space in the Divine Presence. He addressed His servants and asked them, *"Alastu bi-rabbikum*—do you accept Me as your Lord?" Then, *"Qalu, 'Bala"*; at that gathering, each soul declared, "Yes, we accept You."[167] All of them declared that He is the Lord and they promised to worship only Him.

Allah keeps that gathering, and still we are in that Divine Presence and we are giving our respects to the Lord Almighty. No one has moved from that state of being deputy, as Allah honored them and clothed them in that endless honor. From that Day, out of time and space, we are giving our endless respects to Him. Only He can gather. His divine Will is to give His deputies more lights and to make them be crowned with extra lights, *nurun 'ala nur*.[168]

He created man and gave to him from His divine soul, blowing it into him.[169] Originally our soul is from His divine soul. Our physical body, without our soul, is nothing, can't live; it stays alive through our souls. Our

---

[166]O Gatherer of Mankind.

[167]7:172-173.

[168]24:35.

[169]15:29, 32:9, 38:72.

original souls, that Allah clothes with divine deputies' lights, have never yet moved from the Divine Presence. Allah sends, from that soul, only one ray to our physical body, and that is enough to keep it.

He made for us an ability to take more and more lights during this life. We have been created like a river, running from beginning to end, one after the other. Every moment, every second, everything changes; in every unit of time, everything changes, but with our hearts' vision, we are saying that everything is all right. Like a river from Adam to the Day of Resurrection, everyone coming is taking something from Allah's endless favors.

We are coming one after the other and disappearing, and no-mind people are think that whoever disappears from this life is finished, while Allah is declaring to each prophet that only He is *Jami'u-n-Nas*, that He will gather them a second time. No one can disappear finally, forever; no one can hide himself. When He calls, everyone must listen and come and be present in the Divine Presence. And we are waiting for the last stop of this *dunya*. It is not far off.

So many millions went and disappeared from the streets of London; they are only waiting for Allah's invitation and call to them to come. As He gathered everyone at the first, finally, also, on the Day of Resurrection, He will gather everyone in the Divine Presence.

In that gathering, everyone is going to know who is the Seal of the Prophets, who is the first one in the Divine Presence to address his Lord Almighty.[170] He should be called to the Divine Presence, the first to speak and to be addressed.

When He gathers all creatures, He will give His judgment for everyone, putting some people in the direction of Paradise; they will be ready to move. And the second group of people, Allah will give judgment for them for Hells

Then He will address Sayyidina Muhammad ﷺ, the most honored one of all creatures. All people will listen and look and see and understand;

---

[170]This is mentioned in numerous *ahadith* in Bukhari, Muslim and *Mishkat al-Masabih*.

nothing will prevent people's seeing, nothing will prevent them from hearing and understanding. They will have sharp vision and hearing and understanding that Day.

The Prophet ﷺ will come, and all people will look and listen. Allah will make judgment for everyone at the same time. No need to look at the first and second and third, but everyone will think that only he is being judged. (For ladies, men will be judged—long beards! You always kept them back; *now* come on! Ladies will be sitting very quiet and fearful.)

Abu Yazid, Sultan al-'Arifin, knew about his Lord and knew His attributes, and he was saying, "Everyone is afraid of that Day. But I am waiting for that Day to be in the Divine Presence, only to hear my Lord say, 'O Abu Yazid!'—only waiting for that addressing from my Lord to me. Even if He throws me into Hells, seven Hells' fires may even be extinguished from my joy at that addressing!" He was an *'arif,* knowing about his Lord, Allah Almighty.

We are nothing. When Allah says your name, you can't imagine that joy, you should be so happy! Allah created us and gave everyone eyes and noses and cheeks and color. He is working on us and creating, but yet we are not happy, fighting, asking to be another color, also. People are angry with their colors, although He says *"Ahsani taqwim,*[171] so beautiful."

Abu Yazid will be so happy. And you must be happy! If Her Majesty the Queen addressed you, you would be so happy. I am nothing, and if you are really nothing, no judgment for "nothing." Ladies cry quickly, very weak; they can easily be nothing. But you must declare it. The one who says "I am nothing" goes to the right. The one who is "something" goes among the left-wing people.

A person once asked Sayyidina 'Ali ﷺ how Allah Almighty is. Sayidina 'Ali ﷺ said, "For the One who created 'How?' you can't ask 'How?' about Him." No one knows *how* Allah Almighty will give His judgment on the

---

[171]"The most beautiful form." (95:4)

Day of Resurrection.   But He will call to His Throne that one whose name is written on the Throne together with His.

People will look, and Muhammad 🌸 will come and sit on that Throne. And Allah will give the divine Pen to him. Allah Almighty will say, "Now I have finished My judgment for Paradise and Hells. As I said, I did; now, as I promised, My judgment is correct. I am that One who does everything as He likes; no one compels Me, but I compel everything to happen as *I* like. Now I am giving authority to you [Muhammad] and I am saying, 'Take this pen. If you would like to take anyone or everyone to Paradise, you may take.'"

I am the weakest one, and I would take them all. Now one Mercy Ocean is offered to creatures; now it is only the Mercy Oceans of *ar-Rahman*.[172] That Day, *ninety-nine* Mercy Oceans will open to creatures. The Prophet 🌸 will look and see that no one can be out of those Mercy Oceans.

We are happy with our Lord's endless favors! ▲

---

[172]The Most Merciful.

40: the need for spiritual support in our time

The following talk was given on the afternoon of the 27th of Ramadan.

The Night of Power, or the Power of Nights? The holiest night, the Night of Power. When Allah created man weak, He granted to him some means; he may catch them to be powerful. Some of them are material means, some of them spiritual means.

Material means, all of them are only for using temporarily, not permanently. But spiritual powers' sources are going to be for mankind permanently. They may continue throughout their lives, and after this life, also, their power continues.

Men are created weak, and Allah Almighty prepared something for them that they may trust in and continue throughout their lives. If a person feels he is weak, he isn't able to do anything, to act. We are in need to do something and we are asking for something to support us so that we may be able to act.

Allah made so many things on earth which mankind may trust in. Most people are asking for material support; it comes through riches. Everyone likes to be a rich one; no one likes to be poor—a double weakness [for one already weak]! Therefore, people are escaping from poverty and running after power. They think that when they reach to riches, support is perfect. But only for a period.

We are in need of *spiritual* support. Our time is proof that riches do not take away weakness. Maybe that rich person is more weak.

This tape recorder can work on batteries. But there are two openings in each recorder. It means that it can work from the main sources of power, also. If you are in contact with power sources, powers never end.

Material powers are only like batteries; must be finished. But you are created suitable to be connected with heavenly powers. Allah sends some heavenly people, heavenly power sources, and you are suitable to come into connection with those heavenly power sources. That gives you perfect support, never ending.

This point must be well-understood. Don't ask for power through eating and drinking or through riches. The main sources of power are coming from the Heavens, but people have become heedless of those heavenly power sources.

With each prophet, a new channel was opened from heavenly sources. Man is created in the Heavens, not on the earth. Allah could have created him on earth but He did not. Some wrong ideas in other religions say he was created on earth. No! Adam was created in Paradise, to let everyone know that their father was a heavenly being.

When he was sent on earth, he brought his connection, as the first channel of heavenly power sources, to transmit to his children. Adam, when he was ordered to come down on earth, fasted for thirty days, not by breaking fast every day but continuously for thirty days.

He was not like ourselves. When he stood erect, he reached the skies. He heard the glorifying of angels; fear ran through his heart because the angels' glorifying was like thunder. He lived, not dying from hunger after thirty days. It means that he was in connection and heavenly powers were supporting him, even if it were 30,000 days. He was taking from the Divine Presence. And you are also suitable to take from those divine powers!

Therefore, prophets have been sent as extraordinary super-beings. But people are looking at them like themselves; millions of empty-headed people in our time, saying, "What is prophethood? What is the difference between prophets and other people?"

Prophets are sources of heavenly powers. They do not die as we die; [at death] they are only veiled from people, their power never turning off. We are going to be turned off, like engines. If you aren't able to reach to those real Life Oceans among endless Power Oceans, you will die as animals die. *You must ask!*

Now Western people are going to awaken. They are searching for everything. Now, when they have reached a limit of technology, they are asking for something else to reach some other horizons. They can look, but technological means can't take them to those horizons; not possible. They can go up to space from this world, but then how can they reach so many other horizons,?

They sent a rocket towards the skies. There they saw some other things that do not belong to this world and they could not touch them. Some secret knowledge they are still keeping from people. They saw Guardians when that rocket moved around, going at more than their speed—looking, and they were dressed in green. But devils made them not to be known to common people, because devils never like people to believe in something immaterial; they only like them to believe in what they can see.

Can you see what is moving in electric wires or in batteries? Touch them! You can't see, but there is power. Man must believe in the seen and in the Unseen. Allah the Creator sent, by each prophet, a new channel of power. Now, in our times, 124,000 power channels are on.[173] That power is running throughout East and West, North and South, and They[174] are asking to give that power to people.

People are only asking support from riches; as the Last Days approach, people are asking only for material things. But now the end is coming and they are getting in touch with a new era, and that touch is giving them a

---

[173]That is, because at all times there are 124,000 *awliya* on earth, representing the 124,000 prophets who came and went during the course of history, now, as at all times, 124,000 spiritual power sources are open and operating among mankind.

[174]That is, the holy people or saints of Islam who possess such true spiritual power.

new awakening. They are starting to ask for something other than riches, something that gives support. Now they are asking for spiritual powers to support them.

Man must turn to the masters of power on earth. Otherwise, it is so difficult; they should be destroyed by devils. Devils are trying to do that; they are going to do that, within limits. It is going to be a result of heedless peoples' actions; they are preparing their [own] bad ends.

Man must turn to people of power. On the Night of Power during this Holy Ramadan, they have reached new power sources. Each Ramadan Allah re-powers with new powers. On the Night of Power, they have been given double, huge Power Oceans going into action.

Through three and more stations, those powers are going into action. Technology is going to vanish. There should be perfect and complete support for mankind. During past times, no one was in need as we are now. During this Night of Power, there are just appointed huge Power Oceans to be under the control of Sayyidina Mahdi ﷺ. He should be given from both powers, seen and unseen.

The seen affects your body, the Unseen your spiritual body. That power should reach even to those who are under the earth, in graves. When the secret power of the Holy Qur'an appears and is under the control of Sayyidina Mahdi ﷺ, there should be a change for everything, living people or people in graves, for everyone to reach their destinations. They *must* reach their destinations.

We may give only a little drop of knowledge from a huge Ocean to make people understand. It is impossible under these conditions for man to be given more than this, but we hope to reach to that Ocean and swim in it.

As They are giving me to give to you, we hope it should be an honor for you, more than others, that you are listening and believing. And we are thanking our Lord for making an opening for you in a foreign country. Islam is not yet an official religion here. During this holy month, it is an honor for this country, because mercy is falling on them for the sake of these lectures. We hope than no harm harms you and those who belong to you. ▲

41: working toward our main goal: to reach the station of a deputy

Men are created to be deputies, divine deputies on earth. They have been honored.

We have been given a mind or intellect, and our mind is for us like a captain of a ship or plane or train, leading people on to their destinies. Therefore, Islam is established on a mind-base.

Up to a limit, you can use your mind, but mind helps people only within those limits. After those limits, its power finishes. Minds' capacities are within those limits; if you try to use it past its limits, you will destroy it. Beliefs, religions, take people beyond minds.

A difficulty for common people is objecting to something that prophets bring to them. The Holy Qur'an gives explanations on every subject, [including] why people are denying prophets. That must be known.

In the Glorious Qur'an, Allah says that people are denying because they are always asking to use their intellect for understanding. They are asking to understand everything through minds; for everything they are using their minds' knowledge. If anything is beyond their limit, they are saying, "No, we don't accept anything beyond our understanding."

They are mistaken in thinking that there is no understanding and knowledge other than their limited knowledge and intellect. Even our scholars are not yet accepting the knowledge of Sufi people as knowledge. They aren't accepting the knowledge of *tasawwuf*; they are denying *tariqats* and saying, "No more knowledge beyond ours."

How can you make a limit for knowledge whose main source is the endless Knowledge Oceans of Allah, opened to the Prophet 🌹 and from him to his inheritors? I am nothing in that caravan; perhaps I am the last one. But by those grandshaykhs, we have been given authority to make Association with people.

Many times Shaytan is coming and saying, "What are you saying now? You are going to finish!"

And I am saying, "I may finish when my Grandshaykh's knowledge finishes. He may finish when the Prophet ﷺ finishes, and the Prophet's ﷺ knowledge may finish when Allah' s knowledge finishes. Do you think that our main line is going to dry up?"

During the Night Journey, Gabriel reached the limits of the universes, of creation, after which that there is no creation. That is the limit that our knowlege reaches. After that, no one knows except *Hu*.[175]

Gabriel stopped there, but he did not deny what came after those divine territories. The Prophet ﷺ was the only one who was given permission to go further; no one else is permitted to go further.[176] He was the only one, and he was clothed in divine attributes. If not clothed in divine attributes, impossible; no creature could move further. And when Allah asked, "Who are you?" he said, "I am You." "Who are you?" "*You*. No one else except You is here." Absolute Unity Oceans!

A person knocks at another's door. "Who is there?"

He answers, "I am."

"If *you* are there, there is not enough room here for two people. Go away!"

A second time he knocks at the door and that person asks, "Who is there?"

"You!"

---

[175]He, Allah Himself.
[176]Bukhari, 1:345; Muslim, 329.

"All right, come in. There is only place here for one." *Only room for one.* If two is too many, what about three, what about a Trinity?

When the Prophet ﷺ was clothed [by Allah with divine attributes], he finished, and he said, "I am You, You are I." That is the way, if a person approaches that station. And everyone has an ascension. You should reach that station, all of you.

When you reach that station, Allah says, "I am their eyes for seeing and their ears for hearing and their hands for touching."[177] They are reaching the real station of deputies (now we are *candidates* for being deputies).

If They kick this earth, it will take it out of its orbit, throwing the moon far away—deputies' powers. They have been clothed in divine attributes. The Prophet ﷺ was able to see from the front, the back, right, left, up, down, but he saw only Allah.

I am asking scholars if he came back—if, even after he had reached the end of all the universes, he came back in that dress?[178] Allah ordered one ray from his real being to come on earth to his physical body and created a new physical body, going and coming and being with people. The Prophet ﷺ was there in that Divine Presence, never moving.

You have been honored to be a candidate for his deputyhood. But we are asking for something cheap and worthless; no one is interested in reaching that honor. They are denying everything beyond their minds. Our words, only square-headed people can deny, imprisoned in their minds. When they are denying, they are slaves of their egos, of this world, of this temporary life; they are leaving the real life and its pleasures.

The main goal must be to reach the real station of being deputy, not the main goal, business and properties. Those are only little boys' pleasures. Undeveloped people's minds are running after such material goals, such rubbish.

---

[177]Bukhari, 8:509.

[178]The spiritual dress in which Allah clothed him during his Ascension.

The main purpose that you have been given is for ascension; They are waiting to put on your crown to be in the Divine Presence. Grandshaykh said that whoever reaches that, if all the treasures of this world or all the universe were given to him, he would give everything for the pleasure that he will reach in one second of time—*all treasures!* But we are heedless people, never taking care, occupying twenty-four hours with collecting rubbish, and leaving jewels and divine pleasures, that honor for which you can't give any description!

And Allah said, "O My *habib*, My beloved, I am not leaving you alone here.[179] I am clothing your *ummah's* sincere ones in the same dress, and they are going to be with you," those who are following the Prophet ﷺ.

Grandshaykh informed me about a group of people whom the Prophet ﷺ passed after leaving Gabriel—five levels, with 500,000 years between each one and the next. At one of them, he stood and looked, because there were endless Muhammads ﷺ. Allah said, "O Muhammad, I am not making you sit down with people different from yourself, but I am clothing them all like you." No one is going to be sorry that he did not reach the Prophet ﷺ, to give them absolute pleasure. Everyone will look at him, at the Prophet ﷺ and will be given. *You* should be clothed!

That gives information about non-material things for those people who are making it their goal to use ascension and reach to that station. Allah Almighty says, "Those who remain only within their minds' limits are *dhalim*, cruel [to themselves]." That cruelty is destroying them physically and making them suffer, and every difficulty is coming from that, for those who stand only by their minds and do not accept knowledge which is beyond mind.

We are happy to believe in endless Oceans of power, mercy, wisdoms—endless attributes, each reaching to endless Oceans, endless Beauty Oceans, endless Peace Oceans. Only one drop of those Beauty Oceans is enough for eight Paradises; you won't be able to look even at *one* in Beauty Paradises. Gabriel, the most beautiful angel, saw a maiden smiling a little

---

[179]In the Prophet's unique, most highly exalted station.

bit in one place, and her teeth became like lightning. He thought that Allah's Manifestation had come and fell down in *sajdah*, but that maiden laughed and said, "O Gabriel, it is only my smiling!"

Our mother Eve was given, from that maiden's beauty, one drop, and from her beauty-DNA, one drop runs in all women up to today. *What about in the Divine Presence?* Therefore, weekly, on Friday, Allah gives a feast for the people of Paradise. When He opens something from those Beauty Oceans, they forget everything they were given and come to it.

Be happy always, O mankind! Don't follow Satan and devils. A weak servant is calling you. You are free to listen to more, or to devils. Whoever who listens to me should be happy here and Hereafter! ▲

GLOSSARY

Abu Bakr as-Siddiq—the closest of the Prophet's Companions and his father-in-law, who shared the Hijrah with him. After the Prophet's death, he was chosen by consensus of the Muslims as the first caliph or successor to the Prophet. He is known as one of the most saintly of the Prophet's Companions.

Abu Yazid Bistami—Bayazid al-Bistami, a great ninth century wali and Naqshbandi master.

Adab—good manners, proper etiquette.

Allahu akbar—God is the Most Great.

Amir (pl., 'umara)—chief, leader, head of a nation or people.

'Arafat—a vast plain outside Mecca where pilgrims gather for the principal rite of Hajj.

'Arif—knower; in the present context, one who has reached spiritual knowledge of his Lord.

Ar-Rahim—the Mercy-Giving, Merciful, Munificent, one of Allah's ninety-nine Holy Names

Ar-Rahman—the Most Merciful, Compassionate, Beneficent, the most often repeated of Allah's Holy Names.

Astaghfirullah—I seek Allah's forgiveness.

Awliya (sing., wali)—the "friends" of Allah, Muslim saints.

Bait al-Maqdi— the Sacred House in Jerusalem, built at the site where Solomon's Temple was later erected.

Bayah—pledge; in the context of this book, the pledge of a disciple (murid) to a sheikh.

Dajjal—the False Messiah whom the Prophet 靈 foretold as coming at the end-time of this world, who will deceive mankind with pretensions of being divine.

Dhikr (zikr, zikir)—literally, "remembrance" (of Allah) through repetition of His Holy Names or various phrases of glorification.

Du'a—supplication.

Dunya—world, this world's life.

Efendi—Turkish for "sir" or "mister."

'Eid—festival; the two major festivals of Islam are 'Eid al-Fitr, marking the completion of Ramadan, and 'Eid al-Adha, the Festival of Sacrifice during the time of Hajj.

Fard—obligatory.

Fatehah—al-Fatehah, the opening surah or chapter of the Qur'an.

Grandshaykh—generally, a wali of great stature. In this text, where spelled with a capital G, "Grandshaykh" refers to Maulana 'Abdullah ad-Daghestani, Shaykh Nazim's shaykh, to whom he was closely attached for forty years up to the time of Grandshaykh's death in 1973.

Hadith (pl., ahadith)—reports of the Holy Prophet's sayings, contained in the collections of early hadith scholars. In this text, "Hadith" has been used to refer to the entire body of his oral traditions, while "hadith" denotes an individual tradition.

Hajji—one who has performed Hajj, the sacred pilgrimage of Islam.

Halal—permitted, lawful according to the Islamic Shari'ah.

Haqq—truth, reality.

Haram—forbidden, unlawful.

Hasha—God forbid! Never!

Haqq—truth, reality.

Imam—leader; specifically, the leader of a congregational prayer.

Iman—faith, belief.

Jababirah—tyrants, oppressors.

Jinn—an invisible order of beings created by Allah from fire.

La ilaha illa-Llah, Muhammadu rasul-Allah—there is no deity except Allah, Muhammad is the Messenger of Allah.

Maula—master, lord, protector, patron, referring to Allah Most High.

Me'raj—the Holy Prophet's ascension to the Heavens and the Divine Presenc.

Muezzin—one who makes the call to prayer (adhan).

Muluk (sing., malik)—kings, monarchs.

Murid—disciple, student, follower.

Murshid—spiritual guide, pir.

Nafs—lower self, ego.

Nur—light.

Qada wa qadar—the sixth pillar of Islamic faith, referring to the divine decree.

Qiblah—direction, specifically, the direction faced by Muslims during prayer and other worship.

Qiyamah—(the Day of) Resurrection or Judgment.

Rabi'ah al-Adawiyah—Rabi'ah Basri, a great womansaint of the eighth century C.E.

Ramadan—the ninth month of the Islamic lunar calendar, the month of fasting.

Rasul-Allah—the Messenger of God, Muhammad ﷺ.

Sahabah (sing., sahabi)—the Companions of the Prophet, the first Muslims.

Sajdah (also sujud)—prostration.

Salawat—invoking blessings and peace upon the Holy Prophet ﷺ.

Sayyid—leader; also, a descendant of the Holy Prophet.

Sayyidina—our chief, master.

Sayyidina 'Umar—'Umar ibn al-Khattab, the Prophet's eminent Companion and the second caliph of Islam.

Shahadah—the Islamic creed or Declaration of Faith, "Ash-shadu an la ilaha illa-Llah wa ashhadu anna Muhammu rasul Allah, I bear witness that there is no deity except Allah and I bear witness that Muhammad is His messenger."

Shah Naqshband—Grandshaykh Muhammad Bahauddin Shah-Naqshband, a great eighth century wali, the founder of the Naqshbandi Tariqah.

Shari'at/Shari'ah—the divine Law of Islam, based on the Qur'an and the Sunnah of the Prophet ﷺ.

Shirk—polytheism, ascribing divinity or divine attributes to anything other than God.

Sohbet (Arabic, **suhbah**)—the assembly (Association) or discourse of a shaykh.

Subhanallah—glory be to Allah.

Sultan/sultana—ruler, monarch.

Sultan al-Awliya—lit., "the king of the awliya,' the highest ranking saint.

Sunnah—the practice of the Holy Prophet; that is, what he did, said, recommended or approved of in his Companions. In this text, "Sunnah" is used to refer to the collective body of his actions, sayings or recommendations, while "sunnah" refers to an individual action or recommendation.

Takbir—the pronouncement of God's greatness, "Allahu akbar, God is Most Great."

Tarawih—the special nighly prayers of Ramadan.

Tariqat/tariqah—literally, way, road or path. An Islamic order or path of discipline and devotion under a guide or shaykh; Islamic Sufism.

Tawaf—the rite of circumambulatin the K'abah while glorifying Allah, one of the rites of Hajj and 'Umrah.

Ummah—faith community, nation.

'Umrah—the minor pilgrimage to Mecca, which can be performed at any time of the year.

Wudu—the minor ablution that precedes prayers and other acts of worship.

Zakat/zakah—the obligatgory charity of Islam, one of its five "pillars" or acts of worship.

Zakat al-Fitr—the obligatory charity of 'Eid al-Fitr, the festival marking the completion of Ramadan.

Other titles from

Islamic Supreme Council of America

Online ordering available from www.Amazon.com

The Path to Spiritual Excellence
By Shaykh Muhammad Nazim Adil al-Haqqani
ISBN 1-930409-18-4, Paperback. 180 pp.

This compact volume provides practical steps to purify the heart and overcome the destructive characteristics that deprive us of peace and inner satisfaction. On this amazing journey doubt, fear, and other negative influences that plague our lives - and which we often pass on to our children - can be forever put aside. Simply by introducing in our daily lives those positive thought patterns and actions that attract divine support, we can reach spiritual levels that were previously inaccessible.

In the Mystic Footsteps of Saints
By Shaykh Muhammad Nazim Adil al-Haqqani
Volume 1 - ISBN 1-930409-05-2
Volume 2 – ISBN 1-930409-09-5
Volume 3 – ISBN 1-930409-13-3, Paperback. Ave. length 200 pp.

Narrated in a charming, old-world storytelling style, this highly spiritual series offers several volumes of practical guidance on how to establish serenity and peace in daily life, heal emotional and spiritual scars, and discover the role we are each destined to play in the universal scheme.

Classical Islam and the Naqshbandi Sufi Tradition

By Shaykh Muhammad Hisham Kabbani

ISBN 1-930409-23-0, Hardback. 950 pp.

ISBN 1-930409-10-9, Paperback. 744 pp.

This esteemed work includes an unprecedented historical narrative of the forty saints of the renowned Naqshbandi Golden Chain, dating back to Prophet Muhammad in the early seventh century. With close personal ties to the most recent saints, the author has painstakingly compiled rare accounts of their miracles, disciplines, and how they have lent spiritual support throughout the world for fifteen centuries. Traditional Islam and the Naqshbandi Sufi Tradition is a shining tribute to developing human relations at the highest level, and the power of spirituality to uplift humanity from its lower nature to that of spiritual triumph.

The Naqshbandi Sufi Tradition

Guidebook of Daily Practices and Devotions

By Shaykh Muhammad Hisham Kabbani

ISBN 1-930409-22-2, Paperback. 352 pp.

This book details the spiritual practices which have enabled devout seekers to awaken certainty of belief and to attain stations of nearness to the Divine Presence. The Naqshbandi Devotions are a source of light and energy, an oasis in a worldly desert. Through the manifestations of Divine Blessings bestowed on the practitioners of these magnificent rites, they will be granted the power of magnanimous healing, by which they seek to cure the hearts of mankind darkened by the gloom of spiritual poverty and materialism.

This detailed compilation, in English, Arabic and transliteration, includes the daily personal dhikr as well as the rites performed with every obligatory prayer, rites for holy days and details of the pilgrimage to Makkah and the visit of Prophet Muhammad in Madinah.

Naqshbandi Awrad
of Mawlana Shaykh Muhammad Nazim Adil al-Haqqani
Compiled by Shaykh Muhammad Hisham Kabbani
ISBN 1-930409-06-0, Paperback. 104 pp.

This book presents in detail, in both English, Arabic and transliteration, the daily, weekly and date-specific devotional rites of Naqshbandi practitioners, as prescribed by the world guide of the Naqshbandi-Haqqani Sufi Order, Mawlana Shaykh Muhammad Nazim Adil al-Haqqani.

Pearls and Coral, I & II
By Shaykh Muhammad Hisham Kabbani
ISBN 1-930409-07-9, Paperback. 220 pp.
ISBN 1-930409-08-7, Paperback. 220 pp.

A series of lectures on the unique teachings of the Naqshbandi Order, originating in the Near East and Central Asia, which has been highly influential in determining the course of human history in these regions. Always pushing aspirants on the path of Gnosis to seek higher stations of nearness to the God, the Naqshbandi Masters of Wisdom melded practical methods with deep spiritual wisdom to build an unequalled methodology of ascension to the Divine Presence.

The Sufi Science of Self-Realization
A Guide to the Seventeen Ruinous Traits, the Ten Steps to Discipleship and the Six Realities of the Heart
By Shaykh Muhammad Hisham Kabbani
ISBN 1-930409-29-X, Paperback. 244 pp.

The path from submersion in the negative traits to the unveiling of these six powers is known as migration to Perfected Character. Through a ten-step program, the author--a master of the Naqshbandi Sufi Path--describes the science of eliminating the seventeen ruinous characteristics of the tyrannical ego, to achieve purification of the soul. The sincere seeker who follows these steps, with devotion and discipline, will acheive an unveiling of the six powers which lie dormant within every human heart.

Encyclopedia of Islamic Doctrine
Shaykh Muhammad Hisham Kabbani
ISBN: 1-871031-86-9, Paperback, Vol. 1-7.

The most comprehensive treatise on Islamic belief in the English language. The only work of its kind in English, Shaykh Hisham Kabbani's seven volume Encyclopedia of Islamic Doctrine is a monumental work covering in great detail the subtle points of Islamic belief and practice. Based on the four canonical schools of thought, this is an excellent and vital resource to anyone seriously interested in spirituality. There is no doubt that in retrospect, this will be the most significant work of this age.

The Approach of Armageddon?
An Islamic Perspective
by Shaykh Muhammad Hisham Kabbani
ISBN 1-930409-20-6, Paperback 292 pp.

This unprecedented work is a "must read" for religious scholars and laypersons interested in broadening their understanding of centuries-old religious traditions pertaining to the Last Days. This book chronicles scientific breakthroughs and world events of the Last Days as foretold by Prophet Muhammad. Also included are often concealed ancient predictions of Islam regarding the appearance of the anti-Christ, Armageddon, the leadership of believers by Mahdi ("the Savior"), the second coming of Jesus Christ, and the tribulations preceding the Day of Judgment. We are given final hope of a time on earth filled with peace, reconciliation, and prosperity; an age in which enmity and wars will end, while wealth is overflowing. No person shall be in need and the entire focus of life will be spirituality."

Keys to the Divine Kingdom
By Shaykh Muhammad Hisham Kabbani
ISBN 1-930409-28-1, Paperback. 140 pp.

God said, "We have created everything in pairs." This has to do with reality versus imitation. Our physical form here in this earthly life is only a reflection of our heavenly form. Like plastic fruit and real fruit, one is real, while the other is an imitation. This book looks at the nature of the physical world, the laws governing the universe and from this starting point, jumps into the realm of spiritual knowledge - Sufi teachings which must be "tasted" as opposed to read or spoken. It will serve to open up to the reader the mystical path of saints which takes human beings from the world of forms and senses to the world within the heart, the world of gnosis and spirituality - a world filled with wonders and blessings.

My Little Lore of Light
By Hajjah Amina Adil
ISBN 1-930409-35-4, Paperback, 204 pp.

A children's version of Hajjah Amina Adil's four volume work, *Lore Of Light*, this books relates the stories of God's prophets, from Adam to Muhammad, upon whom be peace, drawn from traditional Ottoman sources. This book is intended to be read aloud to young children and to be read by older children for themselves. The stories are shortened and simplified but not changed. The intention is to introduce young children to their prophets and to encourage thought and discussion in the family about the eternal wisdom these stories embody.

Muhammad: The Messenger of Islam
His Life and Prophecy
By Hajjah Amina Adil
ISBN 1-930409-11-7, Paperback. 608 pp.

Since the 7th century, the sacred biography of Islam's Prophet Muhammad has shaped the perception of the religion and its place in world history. This book skilfully etches the personal portrait of a man of incomparable moral and spiritual stature, as seen through the eyes of Muslims around the world. Compiled from classical Ottoman Turkish sources and translated into English, this comprehensive biography is deeply rooted in the life example of its prophet.

The Practice of Sufi Meditation
and the Healing Power of Divine Energy
By Dr. Hedieh Mirahmadi and Sayyid Nurjan Mirahmadi
ISBN: 1-930409-26-5, Paperback. 100 pp.

For those who have reached a level of understanding of the illusory nature of the world around us and seek to discern the reality that lies behind it, Sufi meditation

- *muraqabah* - is the doorway through which we can pass from this realm of delusion into the realm of realities.

This book presents the spiritual background behind the practice of Sufi meditation, then takes the reader step-by-step, through the basics of spiritual connection based on the ancient teachings of the Naqshbandi Sufi masters of Central Asia.

The Honor of Women in Islam
By Professor Yusuf da Costa
ISBN 1-930409-06-0, Paperback. 104 pp.

Relying on Islamic source texts, this concise, scholarly work elucidates the true respect and love for women inherent in the Islamic faith. It examines the pre-Islamic state of women, highlights the unprecedented rights they received under Islamic Law, and addresses the prominent beliefs and prevailing cultures throughout the Muslim world regarding the roles of women in familial, social service and community development, business, academic, religious, and even judicial circles. In addition, brief case studies of historical figures such as Mary, mother of Jesus are presented within the Islamic tradition.